The Sermon and the African American Literary Imagination

The Sermon and the African American Literary Imagination

Dolan Hubbard

University of Missouri Press
Columbia and London

ELMHURST COLLEGE LIBRARY

Copyright © 1994 by
The Curators of the University of Missouri
University of Missouri Press, Columbia, Missouri 65201
Printed and bound in the United States of America
All rights reserved
First paperback printing, 1996

5 4 3 2 1 00 99 98 97 96

Library of Congress Cataloging-in-Publication Data
Hubbard, Dolan, 1949–
The sermon and the African American literary imagination / Dolan Hubbard.
p. cm.
Includes bibliographical references and index.
ISBN 0-8262-0961-0
1. American literature—Afro-American authors—History and criticism. 2. Sermons, American—Afro-American authors—History and criticism. 3. Fiction—Religious aspects—Christianity. 4. Afro-Americans in literature. 5. Christianity and literature. 6. Afro-Americans—Religion. I. Title.
PS153.N5H83 1994
819.9'896073—dc20 94-9968
CIP

∞™ This paper meets the requirements of the American National Standard for Permanence of Paper for Printed Library Materials, Z39.48, 1984.

Designer: Kristie Lee
Typesetter: Connell-Zeko Type & Graphics
Printer and binder: BookCrafters
Typefaces: Palatino, Helvetica Neue, Revue

For permissions to reproduce copyrighted material, see the last printed page of the book.

This book is brought to publication with generous assistance from the John C. Hodges Better English Fund, University of Tennessee, Knoxville.

For Ruth

Aisha

Desmond Jelani

Elizabeth Kendall Hubbard

and to the memory of

Olin Hubbard

Born July 14, 1914

Union County, North Carolina

Died March 13, 1985

Salisbury, North Carolina

The Preacher is the most unique personality developed by the Negro on American soil.

W. E. B. Du Bois, *The Souls of Black Folk*

And unlike white Americans who could assume literacy and familiarity with existing literary models as norms, the slave found himself without a system of written language. . . . He first had to seize the word. His being had to erupt from nothingness. Only by grasping the word could he engage in the speech acts that would ultimately define his selfhood.

Houston A. Baker, Jr., *The Journey Back*

And God stepped out on space,
And he looked around and said:
I'm lonely—
I'll make me a world.

James Weldon Johnson, "The Creation"

Contents

Acknowledgments

The Sermon and the African American Literary Imagination grew out of my deep respect for the richness of black American culture. It is in some measure a tribute to those unsung heroes and heroines who nurtured me in the loving arms of the black church in my piedmont North Carolina hometown, Granite Quarry. It was out of this background that I embarked upon this study.

This book began at the University of Illinois at Urbana-Champaign, where I took my degree in English, specializing in African American literature. I drew on the invaluable advice generously given me by my principal professors at the University of Illinois: Chester J. Fontenot, Jr., Richard K. Barksdale, and Emily S. Watts. The first draft of the book was written during the years 1986–1988, while I was a Carolina Minority Postdoctoral Fellow at the University of North Carolina at Chapel Hill. Special thanks to Charles H. Long, formerly of the Department of Religious Studies at the University of North Carolina, now at Syracuse University, Syracuse, New York. Through his insightful comments, he led me to see the deeper levels of the modes of religious expression of Americans of African descent.

I am especially thankful to Professor Trudier Harris of Emory University, formerly of the University of North Carolina, who encouraged me to continue to seek the higher ground.

Thanks are due to Winston-Salem State University for a Faculty Study Grant and to the University of Illinois for a Graduate College Fellowship. As a 1985–1986 recipient of a National Endowment for the Humanities Fellowship for faculty members at Historically Black Colleges and Universities, I was able to devote full time to the writing of my doctoral thesis.

Access to the libraries of Duke Divinity School in Durham, North

Carolina, Hood Theological Seminary in Salisbury, North Carolina, Moorland-Spingarn Research Center and the Divinity School of Howard University in Washington, D.C., and Walter Royal Davis at UNC–Chapel Hill was invaluable in bringing this project to fruition. I salute Rosemary M. Stevenson, Afro-American Bibliographer and Assistant Professor of Library Administration at the University of Illinois, and Vera M. Mitchell, her very capable Library Technical Assistant, for their assistance, which went above and beyond the call of duty. I am especially grateful to Professor Joseph M. Flora, former Chairman of the University of North Carolina Department of English, for providing me with office space and for generously treating me as a member of the department.

The institutional support of the National Endowment for the Humanities was invaluable, providing me with a summer stipend in 1991, which permitted me to examine sermonic discourse at Yale University and at the Schomberg Collection of the New York Public Library. The University of Tennessee provided me with a grant from the John C. Hodges Better English Fund, which permitted me to further revise my manuscript. I am thankful to Dorothy M. Scura, former Chair, and Allen D. Carroll, Chair, Department of English, University of Tennessee, for their generosity of spirit.

I owe a special thanks to Frances Denise Blue, who meticulously cross-checked my citations. A rising senior at Pembroke State University, she was a participant in the University of Tennessee's Talented Minority Undergraduate Program in 1993.

While the book was in progress, I was sustained by the advice and encouragement of many friends: Adnee M. Bradford, Debra Boyd-Buggs, Mary Kemp Davis, James J. Davis, Thadious M. Davis, Everett Emerson, J. Lee Greene, John O. Hodges, Karla F. C. Holloway, Shanette M. Harris, M. Elaine Hughes, George Hutchinson, Elwanda D. Ingram, Rita and Ronald Kilgore, R. Baxter Miller, Sibyl E. Moses, Floyd and Renda Perry, Betty L. Plummer, Ruby V. Rodney, Rev. Bernard H. Sullivan, Jr., Thelma B. Thompson, and Jerry W. Ward, Jr. To the members of Knoxville's First African Methodist Zion Church, led respectively by Rev. Dr. Michael Ellis and Rev. Alphonso K. Petway, thanks for your tender love.

Finally, my family has been the basic source of my strength—my brothers and sisters, Rebecca, Elaine, Iris, Libby, Tangy, Jvan, Henry, and Henrietta; and my mother- and sisters-in-law, Katherine Hampton, Teresa Torrence, Darlene Hampton, Connie Davis, and Patricia Reid. My wife has been most patient, understanding, and sympathetic. She has been willing to postpone family activities because of my involvement in this study and writing.

I am grateful to all of the persons who have contributed to the development of this research. The work in its final version, however, is my own.

The Sermon and the African American Literary Imagination

1

Toward a Definition of the African American Sermon

O graveyard, O graveyard,
I'm walkin' troo de graveyard;
Lay dis body down.

I know moonlight, I know starlight,
I'm walkin' troo de starlight;
Lay dis body down.

. . . .

And my soul an' your soul will meet in de day
When we lay dis body down.[1]

From the beginning of the modern slave trade, Africans first experienced the New World through the body—the suffocating middle passage, chains, thumb screws, beatings, mutilations, and hangings. Any advantage the Africans gained in their intensified bodily response to their new environment was offset by the loss of their skills as creatively productive and productively creative craftsmen. Alain Locke, one of the first scholars to study the aesthetic underpinnings of black America, believed African Ameri-

1. One of the most popular of the spirituals from the first collection published in the United States is "Lay This Body Down," in William Francis Allen, Charles Pickard Ware, and Lucy McKim Garrison, comps., *Slave Songs of the United States.* John Lovell, Jr., in his *Black Song: The Forge and the Flame,* a sweeping study of the African American spiritual, observes that the persona in this funeral song, "a relic of Africa," contrasts the freedom of the moonlight and starlight against his or her imprisoned body. "Under the guise of a funeral poem," Lovell continues, "he [or she] is stating an unabashed confidence in the ability of life to conquer death" (192–93).

cans retained some memory of beauty, "since by way of compensation, some obviously artistic urges flowed even with the peasant Negro toward the only channels of expression left open, those of song, graceful movements and poetic speech." Stripped of all else, the African American's own body became his prime artistic instrument. So it was the new, oppressive environment that forced African Americans away from their craft arts and their old ancestral skills and toward the emotional arts of song and dance.[2]

In contrast to the "free" dominant culture, black expression begins and ends with the body. The fight for control of the body is rooted in the political. The application of lofty and legalistic "visible" public documents—Mayflower Compact, Declaration of Independence, Constitution, Bill of Rights, Fugitive Slave laws—had a direct impact on these "invisible" people's bodies and bodily movements. To console each other, members of the disconsolate corporate community resorted to those forms of communication that are elemental to mankind: dancing, singing, and speaking.[3]

Having to approach God from a stance different from that of the majority community, black people intuitively recognized the inadequacy of the conventional God-man relationship that formed the basis for much of the Euro-American encounter with God: God speaks, man listens. The black encounter with God has been poignantly expressed as "our fathers/mothers cried and God heard their cries." The revelation of God in the history of the black community was akin to that of the Hebrews in Egyptian bondage, where God said to Moses, "I have seen the affliction . . . and have heard their cry" (Exod. 3:7).[4]

To be sure, the image of the promised land shines brightly as a beacon of hope for Jews, both ancient and modern, and as more than a national dream for most white Americans; nevertheless, it became and has remained for over three hundred years the central theme in the lives of African Americans, who see America as that

2. Alain Locke, *Negro Art: Past and Present*, 3.

3. *The Life and Times of Frederick Douglass*, 146–47. Douglass records a nonreligious ditty that reflects the emergence of a new worldview on the part of the slaves as they respond to how they were defined by the political economy of the New World.

4. See Bercovitch, *The American Jeremiad*, 1–9, and Roberts, "The Black Caucus and the Failure of Theology," 25. Unless stated otherwise, I use the King James Version of the Bible. This passage is from the *Oxford Annotated Bible*, Revised Standard Version.

promised land. And this image of America as the promised land has remained a salient feature of the black American imagination, "despite the fact," as Charles B. Copher reminds us in his sobering observation, "that black Americans did not flee to America's shores from an Egyptian oppression."[5] Unlike the overwhelming majority of Europeans, who saw America as the land of opportunity, Africans, who came in chains, saw America as a land of oppression. White Americans' mighty outward acts of conquest and taming the land required stolen African labor to build the new republic. Black people came to view white oppression as Egyptian slavery and came to sing, "Go down Moses, 'way down in Egypt's land./Tell ole Pharaoh, Let my people go!"

Though the promised land theme occupies the most favored position in black American life, African Americans, as a result of their inverted moral position at the bottom of American society, look at the side of Jesus's ministry that taught kindness to the disinherited with much sympathy. Howard Thurman, the noted philosopher-theologian, stresses that the symbolic universe of the black sermon "is in itself a monument to one of the most striking instances on record in which a people forged a weapon of offense out of a psychological shackle. By some amazing but vastly creative spiritual insight the slave undertook the redemption of a religion that the master had profaned in his midst" by disinheriting black people. Having recovered God as the "center of value," black Americans need not feel that they are approaching God from a theological back door.[6]

Concomitant with the black community's having to turn the moral world upside down in order to stand on theological holy ground is its coming to view history as cyclic. This view challenges and, in fact, inverts the Euro-American linear conception of history, which holds that with hard work the quality of life will progressively get better, that blacks, too, can move into the mainstream. However, the self-evident vestiges of slavery—substandard housing, chronic unemployment and underemployment, and inferior education—are quotidian reminders that for African Americans history is not linear, but cyclic. African American culture was, from the linear perspective, a contrived, bastard culture. The Dred Scott decision de-

5. "Transforming the Land of Oppression into the Promised Land," 25.

6. *Deep River* and *The Negro Spiritual Speaks of Life and Death*, 39–40. See also Olin P. Moyd, *Redemption in Black Theology*, 7, and John E. Burkhart, *Worship*, 16.

fined blacks not as citizens, but as property. This decision had its antecedents in the misguided theology of many mainstream white churches, which defined blacks as people not having souls to save. The Hamitic myth was frequently cited as the scriptural basis for blacks as the racialized Other.[7] As a direct result of their exclusion from full participation in American society, African Americans attempted to redefine themselves and their history through speech acts. Grounded in the church and based to a large extent on improvisation, these speech acts, keyed to the preacher's speech act, provided the aesthetic underpinnings for black oral expression. Forced to creatively imagine their face, black people created a mythology to affirm their tradition as valid and meaningful for all people.

Having had their physical freedom negated, black people developed a view of history that emphasized liberation. Hence, the black sermon in its emphasis on liberation and true Christianity is offered as a corrective to an inadequate history in which black people need not exist, except as beasts of burden. Taking their cue from the preacher, black people used their great critical and creative powers to bring into being a new worldview in which they could readily participate in freedom. Contemporary writers still engage this worldview. Toni Morrison, for example, recovers the myth of the flying Africans in *Song of Solomon*.[8]

The challenge before the preacher-as-creator was, as cultural historian Lawrence W. Levine notes, to invite his spatially immobile community to join him in creating "a new world by transcending the narrow confines of the one in which they were forced to live. They extended the boundaries backward until it fused with the world of the Old Testament, and upward until it became one with the world beyond."[9] It is in this sense that the preacher uses Old

7. Blacks as bastards in the West is a recurrent theme in the works of James Baldwin, e.g., *Go Tell It on the Mountain* and *Notes of a Native Son*. For additional information on the scriptural basis of blacks as the racialized Other, see George M. Fredrickson, *The Black Image in the White Mind: The Debate on Afro-American Character and Destiny, 1817–1914;* Eugene D. Genovese, *Roll, Jordan, Roll: The World the Slaves Made;* and A. Leon Higginbotham, Jr., *In the Matter of Color: Race and the American Legal Process—The Colonial Period.*

8. James H. Cone, *A Black Theology of Liberation*. For a discussion of black people's belief that they could fly back to Africa, see *Drums and Shadows: Survival Studies among the Georgia Coastal Negroes,* 18, 29, 79, 108, 150, 151.

9. *Black Culture and Black Consciousness: Afro-American Folk Thought from Slavery to*

Testament figures such as Isaiah, Jeremiah, and Ezekiel and the New Testament figure of Jesus to comment upon the pain of corporate victimization. The preacher also defines *freedom* as the ability to articulate the self. Through his magnificently wrought oral poetry, the unlettered and semiliterate black preacher, in taking Jesus from *there* to *here* and moving the people from *here* to *there,* moves the spirit of the people beyond the boundary of hierarchical social order to the creation of new forms of human consciousness.

To the extent that the sermon, as well as the other modes of black American expressive culture, enables the preacher and the people to articulate the self, it challenges the dominant culture's ordering of reality (history). Specifically, the preacher and the people contest what M. M. Bakhtin defines as the world of "authoritative discourse," a world that "demands that we acknowledge it [and] make it our own." The "authoritative word," Bakhtin continues, "is located in a distanced zone, organically connected with a past that is felt to be hierarchically higher. . . . It is a *prior* discourse." Unyielding in its demand for our loyalty, the authoritative word demands "our unconditional allegiance. . . . It is indissolubly fused with authority."[10]

It is within this world of "authoritative discourse" that the black preacher must struggle to win his voice and, equally important, an audience that will give assent to his testimony. From an epistemological perspective, the preacher's recovery of the community's voice dictates that he must bind the present to the past while he projects a benevolent cosmology and teleology. Thus, the people see themselves as an extension of history, as both actors and reactors.

In *Understanding the New Black Poetry,* Stephen Henderson sees the "mascon" as the energizing agent in the symbolic universe that issues forth out of black American expressive culture, which is dominated by the emotional sovereignty of the black folk sermon. By "mascon," he means certain "words and constructions [that] seem to carry an inordinate charge of emotional and [spiritual] weight, so

---

Freedom, 32–33. Levine's cogent observation on "the essence of the spirituals" that lies at the heart of the sacred world of black slaves also applies to the authority the community invests in its primary cultural worker—the preacher. See also Paul Radin, "Status, Phantasy, and the Christian Dogma," vi.

10. *The Dialogic Imagination,* 342–43.

that whenever they are used they set all kinds of bells ringing, all kinds of synapses snapping, on all kinds of levels."[11]

The total effect of the mascon clusters, he notes, makes for "complex associations, and thus form[s] meaningful wholes in ways which defy understanding by outsiders." The uninitiated "reads" the sermon (or folklore, blues, jazz) from a superficial or distorted perspective, while the insider sees it as the magnificent constellation in a symbolic universe, functioning within its own boundary. Henderson believes that, collectively, this *"massive concentration of Black experiential [existential] energy* . . . powerfully affects the meaning of black speech, black song, and black poetry."

Rooted in the slave experience, this spiritually and emotionally charged symbolic language is molded by the black experience—one whose central impulse is survival and resistance. In spite of African people's being systematically deprived of their language and of the underpinnings in cultural experience out of which a language comes, the black community was bound together nonetheless by the unifying document of black folk religion.

The Black Sermon as a Culturally Unifying Document

The black sermon is the cultural signature of the children of the African diaspora that fills eye and ear with meanings that dance just beyond the limits of words. The preacher and the people, engaged in a dynamic exchange, transform language as they empty language and fill it anew; that is, they impose through language their moral vision of the world. Replete with drama, the classic black sermon arises out of a richly symbolic context. Hortense Spillers offers a penetrating observation on the grammar of the sermon:

> The thrust of the sermon is passional, repeating essentially the rhythms of plot, complication, climax, resolution. The sermon is

11. *Understanding the New Black Poetry: Black Speech and Black Music as Poetic References,* 44. In his landmark book, Henderson provided the Black Aesthetic Movement with theoretical underpinning. For a critique of Henderson, see Henry Louis Gates, Jr., "Preface to Blackness: Text and Pretext," and George E. Kent, "Reflections on Stephen Henderson's *Understanding the New Black Poetry,* A Review-Essay." See also Dolan Hubbard and Bernard H. Sullivan, Jr., "'Let My People Go': A Spiritually Charged Mascon of Hope and Liberation," 18–28, which discusses how the preacher incorporates the "mascon" to bring social cohesion to the corporate vision.

> an oral poetry—not simply an exegetical, theological presentation, but a complete expression of a gamut of emotions whose central form is the narrative and whose end is cathartic release. In that regard the sermon is an instrument of a collective catharsis, binding once again the isolated members of community.[12]

The preacher taps into the linguistic spaces to bring the community to the point of recognition—the collective catharsis.

Inseparable from the sermon is its geographical and psychological orientation, Africa. One hears in the voice of the preacher the beat of the tom-tom. The preacher's message carries cosmological weight in that it touches people at the core of their being. The black sermon is the communal voice raised in opposition to the reality that the dominant culture chose to make the arbitrary sign of skin color into an ontological distinction. The ostracized community seeks closure first on the social and secular and second on the spiritual and sacred levels.[13] Taking their cue from the preacher, the people break free from economic, psychological, and spatial immobility. The practical purpose of this social discourse enables the people to maintain their dignity and humanity in inhumane situations. Thus empowered, they sing and preach the Lord's word in a strange land. The marvel is that black people sing and preach of their nightmarish experience with such beauty and majesty.

Unlike the traditional Euro-American sermon, which is descended from a learned, literary tradition, the African American sermon is part of an experiential, oral tradition. The black oral tradition utilizes the structure that has become associated with improvisation and jazz but that we know more appropriately can be attributed to

12. "Fabrics of History: Essays on the Black Sermon," 4. Spillers is one of the first students to apply contemporary critical methods to her study of the black sermon. She asserts, quite correctly, that the history of the Afro-American may be read as a "'Jeremiad'—the song of a Fallen man" with the preacher as the chief figure in that drama (2). She examines the sermon within the context of "the *figura* as a system of analysis . . . and the figurative world" (110–11). While we both share a similar interest in how the "performative aesthetics" that came out of the church inform black prose fiction, I see the writers using the sermon as an index that lets us get at the *range* of black American literature. See also Gerald L. Davis, *I Got the World in Me and I Can Sing It, You Know: A Study of the Performed African-American Sermon.*

13. Charles H. Long, *Significations: Signs, Symbols, and Images in the Interpretation of Religion*, 48–51. Long discusses "the manner in which religious phenomena may be interpolated into our lives."

the sermon. This structure reflects the elasticity of African American culture and the African continuum.[14]

Yet, although we can discuss this structure in the sermon, we cannot expect, to paraphrase Edward H. Davidson, a critic to reveal the nature of the black sermon as he/she would reveal the mode of tragedy or that of comedy by reference to *Othello* or *Purlie Victorious.* The essential characteristics of the black sermon cannot be revealed in a single sermon or sermonizer. A sermon by one minister may reveal a sermonic formula or mode that is quite different from a sermon by a different minister. To be sure, a representative sample of black sermons reveals their form or mode; however, the student of the black sermon should be mindful of Martin Luther King, Jr.'s observation that "a sermon is not an essay to be read but a discourse to be heard. It should be a convincing appeal to a listening congregation. Therefore, a sermon is directed toward the listening ear rather than the reading eye."[15] Although King permitted his sermons to be published, he nevertheless had strong reservations about doing so because he knew that the dynamic interplay between the preacher and the congregation has much to do with the composition of a sermon. King was very mindful that the published sermon loses much of its spontaneity, that it is apt to be read as a frozen text.

Christianity with a Black Face

The cultural significance of the historic black church is that it served as a mode of expression. The black church as the "invisible institution" served as a forum for the preacher and the community to perfect in unison the rhetorical modes inherent in the expressive power of black religion. These attendant modes of expression—folklore, blues, spirituals, and style of life—not only addressed who black people were, but they also sustained these "weary travelers" in a strange land as they tried to find a meaningful way out

14. For a critique of the debate between the two principal advocates of the hotly contested African cultural retentions in the United States, E. Franklin Frazier and Melville J. Herskovits, see Albert J. Raboteau, *Slave Religion: The "Invisible Institution" in the Antebellum South,* 48–55.

15. Davidson, "'God's Well-Trodden Foot-Paths': Puritan Preaching and Sermon Form," and Martin Luther King, Jr., *Strength to Love,* 8.

of the American wilderness. Africans in the New World had to come to terms with the gulf that existed between the promise and the practice of Christianity, itself a mode of expression. Herein lies the connection between pulpit oratory and cultural anthropology that we see in these narratives.[16]

Black religion served as an organized way to perfect the rhetorical modes by focusing on the oratory of the black preacher, which was placed in the context of oral Western texts—the prime example being the Bible. Using the church as a forum for organizing black social reality, the preacher thus kept alive the African continuum. Moreover, his drawing upon the call and response of all segments of the church permitted further refinement of the modes of expression.

Although other African American institutions, groups, and individuals emerged to challenge the supremacy of the church (such as schools, fraternal orders and social clubs, burial societies, businesses, and politicians), the black church represents a continuum of the cultural style of black people in its usage of language—modes of playing music, speaking, and writing. These rhetorical modes—keyed to the oratory of the black preacher—set the tone for the creation of self, resolute and free. Within the form and structure of these modes of expression, we can discern the religious orientation of Americans of African descent in the New World. It is in this sense that we can speak of the black church as a "norm." By this, I mean that we see the emergence of a homogeneous style that the aesthetic community recognizes and reinforces through its participation. The black church as the norm cuts across all socioeconomic levels within the community. The culturally sanctioned valences and authority it carries are recognized and appreciated by the churched and nonchurched alike. The preacher-poet-performer as creator of social values must tap into this embedded linguistic code and its attendant responsive mythology if he is to be successful as

16. Commentators on the centrality of the preacher in black life and culture include W. E. B. Du Bois, *The Souls of Black Folk* (1903), Arthur Huff Fauset, *Black Gods of the Metropolis: Negro Religious Cults in the Urban North* (1944), Benjamin E. Mays, *The Negro's God as Reflected in His Literature* (1938), Kenneth Clark, *Dark Ghetto: Dilemmas of Social Power* (1965), Charles V. Hamilton, *The Black Preacher in America* (1972), Zora Neale Hurston, *The Sanctified Church* (1983), and Richard Wright, *Twelve Million Black Voices* (1941).

he *structures* the meaning of blackness. His charge is to awaken dormant cultural values.[17]

The whole matter of cultural values being awakened by a social thinker or prophet has a very rich tradition, from the Old Testament prophets, such as Isaiah, Jeremiah, and Ezekiel, to William Blake, who pictured humanity as a sleeping giant who could be awakened by the correct call to moral responsibility, to Abraham Lincoln, who saw America as abdicating its social responsibility. Likewise Joseph Conrad seems to be touching on the same subject in "Heart of Darkness" when he shows how Marlowe is awakened to the innocence of Africa and the barbarous destruction of the indigenous culture by Kurtz.

But the issue becomes problematic when speaking of a religious figure who awakens values that are dormant, but subsistent, in a culture. The authoritative word of the preacher's discourse does not recognize any other discourse as its equal. The values that the preacher awakens in the people's imagination demand their "unconditional allegiance."[18] These values are there already, for they have served as the underpinnings of the culture. For example, Martin Luther King, Jr., who is the apotheosis of the call to awaken these dormant values, called on Americans to adhere to the primary text to which each American pledges allegiance; this text underpins the culture, yet it was dormant with regard to minorities' rights. Slavery, disfranchisement, segregation, and sexism had made the cultural text dormant and selective, for while Euro-Americans pledged allegiance to the cultural text, they did not mean for one small moment that the text applied to African Americans.

Moreover, when the primary cultural texts were written, there was a tacit understanding that, while the magnificent words of the U.S. Constitution would guarantee freedom from oppression and tyranny for the majority, many of those who signed that document, along with the Bill of Rights, were involved in the negation of fundamental human rights to a large segment of the American population—Native Americans and African slaves. When the Dred Scott decision was handed down in 1857 stating that "black people had no rights that white men were bound to honor," it supplanted the Declaration of Independence and the Constitution as the primary

17. I borrow this concept from James H. Cone, *The Spirituals and the Blues.*
18. Bakhtin, *Dialogic Imagination*, 343.

cultural texts. Hence, perhaps we have two cultural texts in America—the primary text (the pure Constitution and Bill of Rights without the narrative voice of racism) and the implied text of social attitudes and legal disfranchisement that limited the freedoms of minorities.

King, as a prophet, called for adherence to the primary *written* cultural text in which America had invested its morality. The cultural values were already embedded in the American consciousness; they were dormant because whites did not believe that these rights applied to United States citizens of color. King awakened these dormant values by saying, "It is written, and I insist." Echoing the sentiments of anonymous folk preachers, King invited the nation to step out on space and time and join his downtrodden community in making a more humane world.[19]

The black church does not come alive until the preacher calls it alive with the sounds that resonate within his voice. Within the context of the religious orientation of Americans of African descent, the preacher-performer rides the terror as he structures the meaning of blackness. The riding of the terror functions in several ways. First, the preacher encodes the corporate community with a culturally regenerating vision as preacher and community assert their rights to a genuine existence. Second, he both frees the people from the tyranny of man-made states of oppression and equips them to maintain their dignity in demeaning situations. He gives them a sense of being at home in the universe. And finally, the worship service is a self-evident reminder that these invisible people are just as creative in their use of symbols and symbol systems as the dominant culture. This is the unsaid to which Hurston speaks in her elegant, if overstated, aphorism: "All religious expression among Negroes is regarded as art." That the aesthetic community endorses Hurston's observation is expressed in the vernacular with the disarming pejorative "Your musician can't play, your singer can't sing, or your preacher can't preach."[20]

19. Carolyn Calloway-Thomas and John Louis Lucaites, introduction to *Martin Luther King, Jr., and the Sermonic Power of Public Discourse*, 7. I draw many of the details for these observations from a letter Chester J. Fontenot, Jr., wrote to me (March 7, 1990). See also Martin E. Marty, "Martin Luther King: The Preacher as Virtuoso" and Eliseo Vivas, "The Object of the Poem."

20. Hurston, *Sanctified Church*, 83. See also Clifford Geertz, "Religion as a Cultural System," in *The Interpretation of Cultures*, 98–99.

In the culturally regenerating vision of the black sermon, we see belief and theory in action. By this, I mean that the preacher-as-creator recovers Jesus and places Him within the fresh water of the black experience. The preacher's message to his oppressed community is that before there was a *then* or a *there,* a *what* and a *where,* there was God (Ps. 8). The preacher captures the community's sense of metaphysical possibility when he says, as James Weldon Johnson's preacher does in *God's Trombones,* "I'll make me a world." Stepping out on space and time, he brings color and excitement and intensity to an often colorless Judeo-Christian religion. Music is central to the language of the black sermon. The preacher often uses poetic devices to create a musical effect that he utilizes in his delivery. Through his "verbal arpeggios, the cascading adjectives, and the rhythmic repetitions," the preacher transports his oppressed community from the backwaters of the human experience to the breathtaking vision of the Heavenly City.[21]

In his introduction to *Black Preaching,* Henry Mitchell maintains that the "differences in the faith and practice of the various racial, cultural, and theological groups [is] largely semantic." Not one to divorce the black sermon from its cultural context, Mitchell nevertheless recognizes the commonality of the Christian vision. While he acknowledges that the "goal of a raceless church" is very noble, Mitchell is quick to remind us that "years of frustration have crushed the hopeful idea that proof of the unity of all varieties of American Christianity is possible in our time."[22]

I'll Make Me a World

In his signature poem, "The Creation," from *God's Trombones,* James Weldon Johnson captures both the daunting task before the preacher and his passionate resolve to reassure his despised com-

21. Houston A. Baker, Jr., "Belief, Theory, and Blues: Notes for a Post-Structuralist Criticism of Afro-American Literature," 7. Baker discusses the preacher as "the master of metaphor in the Afro-American community." See also Richard K. Barksdale, "Margaret Walker: Folk Orature and Historical Prophecy," 104–17.

22. *Black Preaching,* 11–12. See also John Dillenberger, "On Broadening the New Hermeneutic," 162. On diversity in the Christian faith and the permanence of God's word, Dillenberger succinctly writes: "This . . . does not mean the relativity of all truth, but it does mean that the absolute truth of God is always known to us concretely and appropriately in the forms of the world in which we live."

munity that they are made in the image of God. Johnson illuminates how the black preacher in his unique style demystifies time and allows it to be.[23] The preacher's discourse on "the word" moves from making a cultural statement that is political for black Americans—his call for liberation—to the sublime subject of man's salvation. Drawing on his powers of oratory and his refined flair for the dramatic, the preacher invites the congregation to join him in the making of a world:

> And God stepped out on space,
> And he looked around and said:
> I'm lonely—
> I'll make me a world.

Stepping out of the darkness—itself a symbol of the experience of Africans in America—the preacher imposes a unity of meaning upon what Hayden White refers to as "the chaos of history." The preacher, as archetypal performer, critiques the metaphorical system in which both the blackness of the corporate community and its experiences have been valorized by the dominant culture as a "natural" absence from the historical realm. As a result of this "natural" absence, the black sermon in its totality must be seen as an interjection rather than as a declaration.[24]

Johnson celebrates the sermon as a site of pleasure for the folk preacher and his congregation; he celebrates the preacher for his ability to liberate "the text" from its time-bound meaning as he applies it to the lived experience of his community.[25] The challenge before the preacher as he steps out on space and time is the recovery of voice and vision—with focus on survival, resistance, self-

23. *God's Trombones: Seven Negro Sermons in Verse* (1981). All citations refer to this edition. For a fuller discussion of how the black experience of time informs the work of African American writers, see Bonnie Barthold, *Black Time: Fiction of Africa, the Caribbean, and the United States.*

24. Hayden White, *The Content of the Form: Narrative Discourse and Historical Representation,* 157. See also Henry Louis Gates, Jr., "The Blackness of Blackness: A Critique of the Sign and the Signifying Monkey," 297.

25. William H. Pipes, *Say Amen, Brother,* 156. Pipes advances the notion that, in addition to "the religious motive, the chief purpose of old-time Negro preaching appears to be to 'stir up'; to excite the emotions of the audience and the minister as a means for their escape from an 'impossible world.'" Pipes misreads the extent to which these "black and unknown bards" were instrumental in the creation of a common identity and in the construction of a worldview capable of withstanding the impact of slavery.

actualization, and empowerment (affirmation)—for he must not allow his oppressed community to die spiritually. The preacher's voice becomes the collective voice of his people, who were once "silent" and absent from the historical realm. Through his speech acts, he provides the vehicle by which the entire community of faith may participate in shaping its own history and in restructuring cultural memory.

As the freestanding spokesperson in the community, the preacher was one of the few members of the African American community who was permitted by the politically powerful white community to be educated, self-determined, and successful.[26] The preacher is the transformational agent who walks the critical tightrope between the sacred and the secular; his speech act (sermon) is the agent for historical location. As the tap root of black American discourse, the sermon historicizes the experience of blacks in America. The sermon as agent provides a link between generations of black families and makes it possible for the culture of black America to be transmitted over time and for members of the community to adapt to changing external circumstances, as, for example, in Morrison's *Beloved.*

As Spillers observes, the preacher through his ritual form of expression—the sermon—sings the song of "a Fallen man." With its extraordinary synecdochic power, the metaphor of the Fallen man (with the full archetypal power of this religious paradigm) permeates black American culture. This metaphor celebrates heroic overcoming and achievement. In the process, the preacher articulates the complicated relationship in America between historical memory (jeremiad) and the American Dream (desire).[27]

Here, I am paralleling Houston A. Baker's observation on the blues matrix, "a point of ceaseless input and output, a web of intersecting, crisscrossing impulses always in productive transit," in his *Blues, Ideology, and Afro-American Literature.* Baker's observation on the blues as one of "the culturally specific acts of Afro-American literature and culture" extends those made by James Weldon Johnson in his preface to *The Book of American Negro Poetry.* Johnson

26. Joseph R. Washington, Jr., "Folk Religion and Negro Congregations: The Fifth Religion," 50–59. See also Stuckey, "Through the Prism of Folklore: The Black Ethos in Slavery," 172–91.

27. Spillers, "Fabrics of History," 2. See also Moyd, *Redemption in Black Theology,* 7.

challenged American writers of African descent to embrace the culturally specific of their community. Following his own admonition, Johnson in *God's Trombones* recognized the church as a repository of black cultural expression and the preacher as a primary figure who historicized the experience of blacks in America.[28]

Beyond the majesty and splendor, James Weldon Johnson's *God's Trombones* tells us something more meaningful in what it suggests about the preacher's symbolic significance and the importance of his speech act to the social life of the community. First, his inspired vision represents the distillation of the community's anger, faith, and love. Second, the preacher and the community build a world (the inspiriting congregational dynamic) both to affirm their being made in the image of God and to confront those who challenge their humanity. And lastly, the profound cultural biography, or self-voicing, that asserts itself like a disguised figure in the social fabric of the community testifies to the community's resiliency and determination. The community's privileging of utterance (sermon) under the sign *church* signifies how the black church, the "invisible institution," emerged out of the material/historical condition of black people. It is in this sense that we can speak of the matrix as sermon, the focal point of a network of enterprises whose central objective is the redemption of the black community.

The genius of the black sermon is that it transforms the discrete aspects of black expression from a system of signs, songs, and stories to an oral, expressive, unifying document that conveys a shared value system. The ritualized aspect of the sermon becomes myth—an existential reality—and thus gains social authority to create and disseminate cultural values.[29]

The promise of the black sermon—its message—is that God is at work in all history. The preacher's call to worship is an open invitation for the congregation to participate in an act of creation; their collective construction has as its end result the transformation of reality. As he enters the symbolic universe of the black sermon, the preacher's charge is to renew the community's call for salvation, redemption, freedom, justice, and equality.

28. *Blues, Ideology, and Afro-American Literature: A Vernacular Theory,* 3–4. See also Johnson, preface to *The Book of American Negro Poetry,* 300.

29. Chester J. Fontenot, Jr., review of *The Craft of Ralph Ellison,* by Robert G. O'Meally, 79–80.

Once these dormant cultural values are awakened in the people, the preacher's vision becomes the vision of the community. The preacher who consistently fails to enter this spiritually charged symbolic universe and to awaken these dormant cultural values runs the risk of being publicly ridiculed as one who cannot preach. Numerous interpretations of "your preacher can't preach" exist in the church. These interpretations transcend all religious, educational, and socioeconomic barriers within the black community.

To say that the "preacher can't preach" means that he does not try to merge the historical Jesus and the Gospel with present-day reality so that the message becomes the standard for moral guidance ("Thus saith the Lord!" and not some newspaper or magazine). The preacher revives a system of values that are dormant in the black community. These dormant values are suppressed by numerous sins: pride, avarice, lust, anger, gluttony, envy, and sloth. Through sin, black people separate themselves from true liberation, redemption, confederation, salvation, and hope—and ultimately from themselves. In his sermon, the preacher speaks the familiar themes of sin on two levels, the sacred and the secular. The sacred involves the fractured relationship between God and man, schematized as the previously mentioned seven deadly sins; the secular addresses the sins of inactivity, apathy, and the failure to mobilize to change social injustices.[30]

To say that the "preacher can't preach" means that he does not make the transition between biblical understanding and human conduct (to preach and not to teach). By the proclamation of the word, reality is supposed to get better (i.e., people join the church and/or rededicate themselves to get right with God). The celebratory dimension of black preaching is the church acknowledging in unison that the world is now a better place in which to live.

The sermon moves the people closer to God. A dialectical relationship exists between God and the preacher and the people. By way of analogy, one may equate it with the fluid exchange of a circle flowing through God, preacher, and people. To be sure, many

30. Historically the pulpit fraternity has been seen as a bastion of patriarchal discourse and male privilege. Nevertheless, several black American women succeeded against the odds "to accept the challenge of public ministries." Chief among them were Jarena Lee, Zilpha Elaw, and Julia Foote. See William L. Andrews, *Sisters of the Spirit: Three Black Women's Autobiographies of the Nineteenth Century,* viii.

black preachers complete the circle; however, they do not always complete the vision that is embedded in the linguistic code. Consequently, the preacher can't preach if he does not evoke the vision using the culturally charged language and stylistics. His message neither touches the church member nor moves him/her closer to God and, thus, liberation from sin. The communication between God, preacher, and people during the black sermon will repay careful study by every student of this phenomenon.[31]

The black preacher evokes a profound echo of the early radical Christian rhetoricians (Matthew, Mark, Luke, John). At the heart of black preaching lies authoritative proclamation and joyful celebration, not rational persuasion. Like his biblical counterparts, the black preacher believes the Old Testament doctrine that the speaker is a vehicle of God's will. Something like this doctrine is also found in ancient Greece, where early poets sometimes claimed that the gods spoke through them without conscious effort on their part (as in Hesiod, *Theogony,* 21–35, and Plato, *Ion,* 534d).[32] Thus, the black preacher in his sermon embodies the Aristotelian notion of poet as creator and receiver: what did God say to you? As a result of the black encounter with God, the preacher stands in the prophetic tradition of John of Patmos. He receives a vision from God and communicates it hesitantly. The preacher tells it like it is; he calls the society to repentance as he calls down the evil that threatens to hold black folk back. For example, King created a movement through his rhetoric to address systematic social injustice.

The preacher stands between racism and injustice, and between racism and poverty. He stands between the people and God; his sermon moves people to act more justly in the world as it moves them closer to God. The ethos of black religion is that there is a God somewhere. Du Bois eloquently voices the prophetic dimension of black preaching, where art and thought intersect in the spirituals: "Through all the sorrow of the Sorrow Songs there breathes a hope—a faith in the ultimate justice of things."[33] To say that the

31. Spillers, "Fabrics of History"; Gerald Lewis Davis, *I Got the World in Me;* and C. L. Franklin, *Give Me This Mountain: Life History and Selected Sermons.*

32. George A. Kennedy, *New Testament Interpretation through Rhetorical Criticism,* 6.

33. *Souls of Black Folk,* 213. See also John Lovell, Jr., "The Social Implications of the Negro Spiritual," 128–37. Lovell's observation on the intersection of art and thought

"preacher can't preach" means that he does not complete the communion between preacher, people, and God, that he does not translate the present onto an acknowledgment of his oneness with the people and the experience. In short, he does not powerfully project a benevolent teleology and cosmology.

The form of the black sermon issued directly out of the content of black life. The supreme achievement of the writers under discussion is their use of sermonic language to evoke certain motifs and archetypes familiar to black Americans. Their extensive use of biblical allusions and Christian ritual for symbolic expression have black religion as a point of spiritual departure to tell the tragic but heroic story of black people's lot in America.[34]

In this study, I intend to offer a hermeneutical discourse on the modes of religious expression that developed out of the African encounter with the New World and to investigate how these modes of expression have been transformed into the scribal tradition and have influenced the structure as well as the theme of selected works of black American prose fiction. Using the rhetorical modes that developed out of the black church as points of reference, I will examine the extent to which the dynamic exchange between sacred language (the sermon) and secular modes of expression (blues, jazz, political speeches) manifests itself in the narrative configuration; the extent to which these modes generate narrative structure and character development, texture of language and imagery; and the manner in which language itself creates a vision of an African American perspective toward history.

This outline of the course of the African American sermonic tradition is central to the creation of a black identity. I begin with the notion that the African American sermonic tradition is grounded

---

in the spirituals applies also to its homiletical twin—the sermon. In discussing the social impact of the spiritual, he lists three elements as the leitmotif of most spirituals. They are, first, "the Negro's obsession for freedom," second, "the slave's desire for justice . . . upon his betrayers," and third, "the strategy . . . to gain an eminent future" (136–37).

34. On how the preacher uses the symbolic language of the black sermon to mobilize the community, see Chester J. Fontenot, Jr., "Visionaries, Mystics, and Revolutionaries: Narrative Postures in Black Fiction," 63–87, and Martin Luther King, Jr., *Stride toward Freedom: The Montgomery Story*, 290–92. See also Peter L. Berger and Thomas Luckmann, *The Social Construction of Reality: A Treatise in the Sociology of Knowledge*.

in a self-consciously shared vision and that understanding this vision is essential to appreciating the consistent themes and patterns of African American literature. My concept of religion does not set at odds the church (sacred) to the extrachurch (secular) as though the holy and the profane are two sharply delineated spheres. On the contrary, it is my judgment that, while the sacred and the secular are distinct, the African American tradition sets amorphous and permeable boundaries between the two modes. Religion, Andrew M. Greeley says, "is part of daily life anterior to and more important than the trappings which ecclesiastical institutions add to it."[35]

The challenge before the black prose fiction writer is to transform historical consciousness into art, to use it as a strategy for representation, and to merge it with the political as he or she presents the emergence of a self. In the synoptic discourse represented by the closely repetitive strands, familiar tropes, and mythic themes, the challenge before black prose fiction writers is one of infinite possibility as they come to grips with the enslavement of Africans in the New World. Moreover, the conjunction of the writer's and the preacher's voices attests to the validity of the experience as the writers articulate the central character of the experience for the corporate community. They offer insights into the relationship between the preacher's ritual form of expression—the sermon—and black people's position in American society.[36]

The writers under discussion are the recipients of a doubly rich heritage—the black oral tradition and Western texts, the most important of the latter being the King James Bible. Their philosophy of art fits into the structure of Christian eschatology: the preservation of the spirit beyond the flesh. However, these writers know that Christian explanations have never proved quite adequate for blacks, whose sensibilities are deeply rooted in folk traditions. They convert this tension between black oral tradition and Judeo-Christian moral absolutes into an operative principle of black art.

Their use of the language of religion to tell the story of a fallen people represents absorption into a discourse that is recognized by the aesthetic community—a discourse that antedated and shapes

35. *Religion: A Secular Theory,* 1–2.

36. Blyden Jackson, "The Ghetto of the Negro Novel: A Theme with Variations," 100. Jackson asserts that "the world of Negro fiction is as static as the world of the medieval synthesis."

their voice and vision. Their use of the language of religion says to the world that there is something of intrinsic worth, beauty, and dignity within the community, over and above the culture of oppression. They share, as Arif Dirlik observes, an ideology that "is consonant with the fundamental activist epistemology that underlies [their] work as a whole. . . . [They see tradition] as an activity in the production of a past that is rooted in the social struggle over hegemony."[37] They use the language of religion as entrée to a critique of the church as the dominant social institution that emanated from the culture of oppression.

With differing degrees of emphasis, they see the language of religion as both limiting and liberating, both powerful and repressive, as the Barbee-Trueblood episode in Ralph Ellison's *Invisible Man* shows. As ideological practice, Barbee's sermon counsels a conservative approach as a solution to the problem of black oppression, while Trueblood's life refutes Barbee's underlying notion of progress. The power that flows from the church masks other contradictions that exist in the community, such as patriarchal power and sexist practice. This constitutes the narrative tension that often makes the text seem to be at "war" with itself.

The challenge before these writers is to work out the dynamic exchange between the church and extrachurch modes of religious expression. They set up a dialogue of voices, as well as forms, as they respond in their own work to their predecessors on many African American themes: the quest for freedom and literacy, the search for identity and community, the need to humanize an antagonistic white world by giving it a black face, the lure of upward mobility, the fictionalizing of history, and the use of romance to

37. "Culturalism as Hegemonic Ideology and Liberating Practice," 26. For a more dialectical treatment, which highlights the liberating and debilitating aspects of the Black Christian Churches, see Genovese, *Roll, Jordan, Roll.* See also Ronald Gerald Palosaari, "The Image of the Black Minister in the Black Novel from Dunbar to Baldwin." Palosaari concludes that black novelists have rejected the ministry as a distasteful racial role into which the black man in America is so often pushed. Yet many of these same writers are captivated by the artistry of these men of words, and this is as it should be. The black church provided black people with a language for articulating the self in a hostile world. What many black writers find *distasteful* is evangelistical Christianity's hegemony over the life of the mind. Clothed in a folk view of Calvinism, it espouses an anti-intellectual individualism and depicts blacks as loyal, faithful servants. Also see Walter C. Daniel, *Images of the Preacher in Afro-American Literature.*

transform an oppressive history into a vision of mythic transcendence. In summary, I propose to examine how the writers under discussion use the rhetorical forms of the black preaching style, with its attendant expressive power, to bring readers to the point of recognizing their characters' symbolic importance.

Like black preachers, black fiction writers work within the cultural biography and cyclic history of black America to describe a world that is meaningful to blacks. I do not attempt to exhaust the field of black fiction works that make use of sermonic practices and features. My task, as I see it, is to help open critical territory, not prescribe its boundaries. Hence I focus on selected writings of Frederick Douglass, Frances Ellen Watkins Harper, Paul Laurence Dunbar, Zora Neale Hurston, Ralph Ellison, James Baldwin, and Toni Morrison.

The very idea of examining the sermon and the African American literary imagination means that one must acknowledge the political conservatism of black religion—its tendency to promote a submission to authority in the face of subversive impulses of the will.[38] An irreconcilable tension exists between those members of the community who advocate a theology of love and those who advocate a theology of anger. This tension over how best to achieve racial equality in America generates pressures that often call into question the moral integrity of the preacher's leadership.

Some black religious leaders have allied themselves too closely with white benefactors and patrons. They advocate a sociopolitical conservatism and thereby run the risk of having their loyalty to the community's call for social justice questioned. Others have identified themselves with the anger of the black community and have communicated their anger in their rhetoric and action. Set over and above the practical problems of racism, the fight for social justice and economic equality, the black preacher, regardless of his ideological bent, is charged with bringing "de Word."[39]

Although the writers under discussion may be distrustful of the preacher's intent, they nevertheless are attracted to him for his ability to call the world to order and his ability to manipulate "an

38. Genovese, *Roll, Jordan, Roll,* 161–69.

39. Peter J. Paris, *Black Leaders in Conflict: Joseph H. Jackson, Martin Luther King, Jr., Malcolm X, and Adam Clayton Powell, Jr.,* 16. See also Hamilton, *Black Preacher in America,* and Gayraud S. Wilmore, Jr., *Black Religion and Black Radicalism.*

interworked system of construable signs" to make manifest that which is concealed from the community in day-to-day experience.[40] For example, it is clear that Ellison's unnamed protagonist aspires to become a productive member of the American mainstream and to be free of the institutional forces opposing him in his pursuit of life, liberty, and happiness. Having his aspirations blocked, the nameless narrator draws upon the cultural specificity of the sermon to dissolve his opacity and to reveal his normalcy.

The Dialectical Tension in the Secular and Sacred Visions

Charles H. Long, a historian of religions, challenges students of African American culture to expand their own consciousness by examining the full range and diversity of the religious orientations of black Americans. He reminds us that African American religious codes extended beyond the Christian faith and that "not all the religious meanings of the black communities were encompassed by the Christian forms of religion. . . . Some tensions have existed between these forms of orientation [folklore, music, style of life] and those of the Christian churches, but some of these extrachurch orientations have had great critical and creative power. They have often touched deeper religious issues regarding the true situation of black communities than those of the church leaders of our time."[41]

The creators of this religious worldview respected the robust uncertainty of life; they understood that good and evil, creative and destructive, wise and foolish, up and down, were inseparable polarities of existence:

Sometimes I'm up
Sometimes I'm down
Oh, yes, Lord.[42]

Coexisting with this attitude, "so un-Anglo Saxon in its balance and complexity,"[43] is the blues modality that speaks of the agony of

40. Geertz, *Interpretation of Cultures,* 14.

41. *Significations,* 7.

42. Lerone Bennett, Jr., *The Negro Mood,* 50–52. Bennett reminds us of the Saturday night/Sunday morning dialectic of the blues and spirituals. See also Richard Wright, "The Literature of the Negro in the United States," 85–90. The songs are quoted from *Negro Mood.*

43. Bennett, *Negro Mood,* 51.

life and of the possibility of transcending it by sheer toughness of spirit:

> I got the blues
> But I'm too damned mean to cry.

A consistent theme running throughout these sacred and secular forms of religious orientation is the degree to which black people judged not only themselves and the white man, but also God.

In *The Souls of Black Folk,* Du Bois regards the inherent tension in these two perspectives as the backside of the black religious encounter with God. Black people must be ever vigilant and stand guard against the seductive powers of this "deep religious fatalism."[44] The sublime simplicity of spirituals such as "Nobody Knows de Trouble I See" and "All God's Chillun Got Wings" artistically expresses the deep-seated spiritual tension that has for over three hundred years dogged the African encounter with America. The communal mood swings back and forth, on the one hand, between despair and optimism and, on the other hand, between resignation and redemption. These rhythms of faith are but the outward manifestation of the deep-seated cultural angina resulting from the recognition that, for African Americans, the land of oppression has not become the land of promise.

I am interested in the way in which the church and extrachurch modes of expression come to terms with the oppressive nature of the religious experience as well as with the anger, resentment, tension, isolation, frustration, and echoes of hate and revolt produced by man-made oppression. It is in this sense that I maintain that the church and extrachurch modes of expression are colored by a blues sensibility, if by *blues* one means the working out of the tension between what Richard Wright in "The Literature of the Negro in the United States" refers to as the sensualization of pain and pleasure as opposed to the transcending of pain and pleasure.[45]

One sees evidence of the dialectical tension that exists between secular (blues) and sacred (spirituals) vision in the structure of Dante's *Divine Comedy.*[46] Dante's hero, Virgil, immerses Dante in

44. *Souls of Black Folk,* 162.
45. Wright, "Literature of the Negro," 88–89.
46. Dante's greatest work, *The Divine Comedy,* begun about 1300, has traditionally entitled him to rank among the great poets of all time. Dante called his poem the

the blues structure (hell, suffering, pain) as penitence for his sins and the collective sins of all of Christian tradition. The spiritual vision in *Divine Comedy* comes when Dante surrenders his human reason to divine grace. This act allows him to perceive the will of God and enter the eternal bliss of heaven. Within the African American literary tradition, there are several narratives that play upon Dante's myth, such as Amiri Baraka's (née LeRoi Jones) *The System of Dante's Hell,* Alice Walker's *The Color Purple,* and Gloria Naylor's *Linden Hills.* Structured on the themes of Dante's *Inferno* (violence, incontinence, fraud, treachery), these works describe the experiences of blacks in America—lost souls trapped in the American Dream.

When pondering the phenomenology of race in his masterpiece, *God's Trombones,* in relation to black people's sense of self or the black writer's sense of well-being, Johnson both establishes a firm basis for our celebrating the oral expressive forms rooted in the black church and challenges us to plumb these speech acts for what they tell us about the ambiguity and irony of black life. Johnson thus inaugurated a tradition in African American letters in which succeeding generations of writers would have to come to grips with the oratory of the black preacher as an informing feature of black literature.

Likewise, the writers who utilize this tradition invite their readers to join them in the making of a world. I am particularly interested in the changes that occur in this improvisational, oral form when it is transformed into a written form within the African American literary tradition. What is involved in its literary production are subtle differences in the sermon's manifestation and context as a form of thought in language.

The "full" concretization of the sermon/text is realized when the embedded cultural referents explode in the imagination; at that moment, the preacher/writer and the audience are one. The sermon/text serves as cathartic release from the tyranny of the everyday. Re-

Commedia; the epithet *Divina* was added some two centuries later. A comedy only in the medieval sense of having a fortunate ending, the poem describes the experiences of the human soul after death; Dante recounts his own pilgrimage—under the tutelage of the Roman poet Virgil—through Hell and up the mount of Purgatory, until at last he arrives in Paradise, where he is welcomed by the soul of his idealized Beatrice.

energized, preacher and people, writer and reader celebrate the indefatigable human spirit and confront an exploitative ideology. Alert to the demands of their aesthetic community, writers in their literary performances, no less than preachers in their oral performances, are thoroughly implicated in the demand for participatory response from their readers to their narratives. In regard to the writers under discussion, Baldwin, perhaps, sermonizes (anticipates the demands of his aesthetic community) more authentically than the others; however, this is not to say that Hurston, Ellison, or Morrison are less authentic. I suggest that they occupy different positions on a sacred-secular continuum. For example, Baldwin tends toward the sacred pole; Ellison tends toward the secular, or extrachurch. But the cultural authority invested in the black sermon is so deeply embedded in the black psyche that, whether one be preacher, pimp, or poet, one's status in the black community is often measured by how fluent one is in this collective, communal oral literature. The black sermon is the heroic voice of black America.

2

Sermonic Hermeneutics in Early Black Narratives

The Preacher is the most unique personality
developed by the Negro on American soil.
W. E. B. Du Bois, *The Souls of Black Folk*

The common point of origin for much black fictional and nonfictional prose resides in that most unique of American genres: the slave narrative. Wrapped in compelling melodrama, its blend of oratory, chanted songs, and rhythmic sermons caught the imagination of freedom lovers everywhere. While much attention has been paid to the messianic leitmotif, to the quest for freedom and literacy, and to scenes of reading and writing as common rhetorical structures that bind the texts as genre, little critical attention has been paid to the writers' use of sermonic rhetoric and how they invoke and subvert this rhetoric in their texts to produce what John F. Callahan refers to as "the spoken in the written word."[1]

Frederick Douglass's 1845 autobiography, *The Narrative of the Life of Frederick Douglass, An American Slave, Written by Himself,* as Valerie Smith observes, "owes its importance in part to the subtlety of the narrative voice": Douglass's ability to counterpoise black oral culture against that of scribal tradition. By representing the conflict of his desire to be a man and an American against an intransigent

1. "Chaos, Complexity and Possibility: The Historical Frequencies of Ralph Ellison," 130–38, and Robert G. O'Meally, "Frederick Douglass' 1845 *Narrative:* The Text Was Meant to Be Preached"; for additional commentary on the messianic leitmotif, see Harding, *There Is a River;* on scenes of reading and writing, see Houston A. Baker, Jr., *The Journey Back: Issues in Black Literature and Criticism.* Callahan, *In the African-American Grain,* 25.

America's determination to maintain the "color curtain," Douglass's incorporation of black oratory captures the dialectical tension between the interests of black and white America.[2]

With Douglass's narrative as their referent, the early black prose fiction writers' works decry the color curtain and simultaneously de-emphasize black oral culture. Where the oral culture breaks through in terms of voice and vision (narration), we can discern in the work of literature "its relation to politics and to ideology through the positioning of characters."[3] Moreover, the early black prose fiction writers' depiction of the minor characters, including the preacher, serves as a cultural clue in the struggle for the soul of black America.

I intend to explore how Frederick Douglass integrates the "preacherly voice" into his 1845 *Narrative* and to briefly examine the problematics of this preacherly voice for writers of early black prose fiction, such as Frances Ellen Watkins Harper and Paul Laurence Dunbar. As Bernard Bell observes, the underlying tension in their novels stems from their difficulty in transforming folk culture into "'high' culture as the standard of moral and spiritual humanistic achievement [to validate] the moral authority and spiritual wisdom of folk culture itself." Specifically, I refer to the way the community organizes and preserves human knowledge and traditions that it considers important. This tension crests with the third generation of black novelists.[4]

At a deeper level, the language of religion in their fiction may be read as the embodiment of desire; it is a substitute for the community's lack of economic parity, as is evident in the spiritual "You May Have This World, But Give Me Jesus."[5] By assigning the folk forms to the masses, the writers muted the connection between art

2. *Self-Discovery and Authority in Afro-American Narrative*, 1.

3. Ibid., 7.

4. Bernard Bell, *The Afro-American Novel and Its Tradition*, 76.

5. Herman Dreer, *The Immediate Jewel of His Soul*. In his lone novel, Dreer uses the exasperation captured in this spiritual to comment on the economic inequality that separates black from white America. The Reverend William Smith, his socially minded protagonist, preaches: "The masses of us [have said] 'You may have all the world, but give me Jesus.' True, we have Jesus and the white people have the world. Who is the happier?" (53) For a discussion of Rev. Smith as the embodiment of "the most anti-clerical minister in the Negro novel" (90), see Palosaari, "Image of the Black Minister," 89–91.

and power; therefore, they deprived their literary productions of their authority as fictions of power. However, a closer inspection of their rhetorical structure suggests that they recovered the mythic vision in the religious connotation they attached to certain words, such as *freedom* and *land,* and to themes such as "faith" and "redemption" in America. They worked through the Christian myth to tell their story.

While these writers unearthed no new configuration of character and intent in the African American mind-set, they served as a very sturdy cultural bridge, paving the way for the various literary awakenings in the 1920s. A generation of writers sufficiently removed from the sociocultural pressures of the post-Reconstruction period then affirmatively began the inward turn to explorations of self and society.

Lord, I Want to Be a Christian in-a My Heart

Shaped by the religious imagination of the black church, a church that provides him with a model and a language for meeting the world, Douglass, in his 1845 *Narrative,* with seemingly effortless motion, points the way for future generations of African American writers to mine the oral expressive tradition of black America. His narrative is a prime example of how black oral expression takes generic shape in the slave narrative, where the issue of defining self and finding a voice assumed paramount importance. As Houston A. Baker notes, "Only by grasping the word could [Douglass] engage in the speech acts that would ultimately define his selfhood." Like the black preacher, Douglass creates a space out of no space as he makes himself a world.[6]

Although Douglass locates his narrative at the heart of our still unresolved conflicts about race and about property versus contrasting values, he draws on the rhetoric of the black preacher as he articulates the basic unresolved conflict of the status of blacks—as a commodity, a black, and a human being. In the process, he illumi-

6. Baker, *Journey Back,* 31. The mining of the oral expressive forms, including sermonic rhetoric, had to wait until blacks gained enough distance from the slave experience, which began in earnest during the literary awakening in the early part of the twentieth century by writers such as James Weldon Johnson, Jean Toomer, Langston Hughes, and Zora Neale Hurston.

nates the fractured relationship between God and humanity schematized as racism. Moreover, he illuminates the need for community in a fragmented, acquisitive American society. Douglass saw this rapaciousness as a real threat to genuine community. Through his portrait of white people corrupted by slavery and blacks crippled by racism, Douglass shows us how the principle of community itself is undermined, which anticipates "class tensions" in the early black novel, as we shall see.[7]

That an African American aesthetic tradition informs Douglass's *Narrative* becomes apparent when we examine the role of religion during his formative years. Indeed, long before Douglass became the central character in his *Narrative,* God was the central force in his life. His religious life was awakened when he was thirteen. In his *Life and Times,* he movingly recounts the steadying influence of the pious and semiliterate "Father" Charles Lawson, his spiritual tutor, who lived near Master Hugh Auld in Baltimore. Lawson, a free black, was a drayman for rope-maker James Ramsey and a devout member of the Bethel African Methodist Church, which Douglass also joined. Douglass wrote: "I went often with him to prayer-meeting and spent much of my leisure time on Sunday with him. The old man could read a little, and I was a great help to him in making out the hard words, for I was a better reader than he. I could teach him 'the letter,' but he could teach me 'the spirit,' and refreshing times we had together, in singing and praying."[8]

Father Lawson is a sterling example of those slaves who, as Gayraud S. Wilmore notes, "possessed great self-esteem and confidence in their own manner of believing and worshiping God."[9] These unsung heroes and heroines polished the leadership, ability, and other talents of generations of blacks for frontline duty. And Lawson, like countless other unsung heroes, saw something in Douglass that Douglass himself did not see: "The good old man had told

7. Robert Shulman, "Divided Society, Divided Selves: 'Bartleby, the Scrivener' and the Market Society," in *Social Criticism and Nineteenth-Century American Fictions,* 4, 6–27. In his 1845 *Narrative,* Frederick Douglass anticipates themes Mark Twain would use thirty years later in *Huckleberry Finn.* See also David Grimstead, "Melodrama as Echo of the Historically Voiceless," 82–83.

8. *Life and Times* (1962), 90.

9. *Black Religion and Black Radicalism,* 11.

me that the Lord had great work for me to do, and I must prepare to do it; that he had been shown that I must preach the gospel. His words made a very deep impression upon me, and I verily felt that some such work was before me, though I could not see how I could ever engage in its performance."[10] Here, Douglass, with studied understatement, downplays his spellbinding "performances" before the antislavery audiences.

For Douglass, the nation was his pulpit. The two-part text of his *Narrative* could easily have been titled: "How do you make a man a slave and then a man again?" To this end, his sermon builds toward its climactic moment: Douglass's fight with the noted slave breaker Covey. Douglass's larger design is to lacerate the consciousness of the backsliding young republic. His message is a stern reminder that it must not abdicate its moral responsibility in regard to the enslavement of four million people of African descent.[11]

His first two chapters, with their matter-of-fact description of the world of the slave, serve to introduce themes and motifs that will recur throughout the narrative, and to implicitly introduce the first part of his text: "How do you make a man a slave?" Themes and motifs that Douglass treats include the world of the slave as hell, the motherless child as child of God metaphor, the dehumanization of master and slave, and the ethos of the slave community that emerged to counter the dehumanizing slave-making process.[12]

Douglass, a past master of the dramatic art of storytelling so characteristic of the folk preacher, casts himself as the central character in his riveting drama. Appropriately, this black Everyman's first vivid image of what it means to be a slave is the unmerciful assault on black womanhood. He is forced to watch the relentless beating of his attractive aunt for seeing the man of her choice. That which the white woman prizes is violently denied her dark-skinned sister. Implicit in his description is the utter powerlessness of black men to protect their women. The deep impression is made upon the

10. *Life and Times*, 91.

11. For an account of Douglass's famous "slaveholder's Sermon," which he gave often during his youthful days as an abolitionist lecturer, see "The Southern Style of Preaching to Slaves" in *Speeches, Debates, and Interviews, 1841–1846*, 15–17.

12. On the dehumanizing slave-making process, see Douglass's "Reception Speech" at Finsbury Chapel, Moorfields, England, May 22, 1846 (misdated May 12), in *My Bondage and My Freedom;* also in *Speeches, Debates*, 1:269–99.

five- or six-year-old Douglass that the world is, indeed, a most unfriendly place:

> I remember the first time I ever witnessed this horrible exhibition. I was quite a child, but I well remember it. I never shall forget it whilst I remember any thing. It was the first of a long series of such outrages, of which I was doomed to be a witness and a participant. It struck me with awful force. It was the blood-stained gate, the entrance to the hell of slavery, through which I was about to pass.[13]

Douglass's authorial posture is that of a defenseless child alone in the world. The narrative progression builds from truncated childhood to rebellious, strapping young manhood. Undoubtedly, spiritual disorientation was the intent of the slave system in order to permit the masters to usurp the position normally occupied by God. In a larger sense, Douglass is the lonesome pilgrim, the motherless child a long way from home, trying to keep his wits about him and make sense of a world turned upside down, where right is wrong and wrong is right. In effect, the slave community functions as his surrogate parent.

In his *Life and Times,* Douglass reveals that Miss Sophia, the model of Christian charity, for several months acted as a surrogate mother. In his *Narrative,* she stands in stark contrast to Douglass's vivid descriptions of such "soul killers" as the wicked owners and vicious overseers. Immediately attracted by her kindness, Douglass fondly recalls the warmth she engendered: "She was entirely unlike any other white woman I had seen. . . . Her face was made of heavenly smiles, and her voice of tranquil music" (57). Without a doubt, she is the star attraction in Douglass's parable on learning to read.[14]

Miss Sophia is the exemplar, the quintessential example of how

13. *Narrative,* ed. Benjamin Quarles, 28. All citations refer to this edition and are hereafter noted by page numbers in parentheses.

14. A review of Douglass's genealogy reveals him to be a cousin by marriage to Miss Sophia. Lucretia Planner Anthony (1804–1823), who, as the youngest child of Aaron Anthony—reputed to be Douglass's father—was believed to be Douglass's half sister, married Hugh Auld's brother, Thomas, who sent Douglass from the eastern shore to Baltimore (Dickinson J. Preston, *Young Frederick Douglass: The Maryland Years,* 3–8, 91). On balance, Miss Sophia became a surrogate mother figure in Douglass's early life. He indicates as much in his *Life and Times* (77), an expanded version of chapter 6 of his *Narrative.*

slavery stains the soul and stamps out basic kindness and gentility. Her benign disposition soon evaporates when Mr. Auld finds out that she has begun to instruct Frederick in the fundamentals of language. He vehemently objects with a ringing denunciation that "learning would *spoil* the best nigger in the world" (58). Douglass sadly notes that Miss Sophia, an energetic convert to the religion of the slavemaster, had had a "lamblike disposition [that] gave way to one of tiger-like fierceness" (64).

Her change of heart is too late, for in the twinkling of an eye, Douglass had divined, "by the merest accident" (59), the power of the word. He understood the process through which the subjugation of the slave is achieved. His imagination leaped beyond the boundary of its assigned space in contemplation of other possibilities:

> These words sank deep into my heart, stirred up sentiments within that lay slumbering, and called into existence an entirely new train of thought. It was a new and special revelation, explaining dark and mysterious things, with which my youthful understanding had struggled, but had struggled in vain. I now understood what had been to me a most perplexing difficulty—to wit, the white man's power to enslave the black man. (58–59)

This unexpected revelation does much to determine Douglass's course of action, for he resolves "at what cost of trouble, to learn how to read" (59). Informed of the tools necessary to challenge his structurally silent position, he pledges to free himself from "the prison-house of language":[15] "What [Mr. Auld] most dreaded, that I most desired. What he most loved, that I most hated. That which to him was a great evil, to be carefully shunned, was to me a great good, to be diligently sought; and the argument which he so warmly urged against my learning to read, only served to inspire me with a desire and determination to learn" (59).

Douglass concludes his parable with self-enfolding ironies. The slave was constantly told that he or she was a brute, without a meaningful past and without a system of written language. Douglass, too, had accepted these definitions; yet, in the creation of self from nothing, he contests those who would define him, as the

15. Fredric R. Jameson, *The Prison-House of Language,* 89. In "Of Our Spiritual Strivings," the first chapter in *Souls of Black Folk,* Du Bois equates being black with living in a prison.

balanced antithesis of the passage indicates. The irony is that people like Mr. Auld, who would superimpose "the cultural sign *nigger* on vibrant human beings" like Douglass, are themselves defined by Douglass—this beast of burden. By converting their otherness into discourse, Douglass becomes master of his own situation. Thus, he makes the very people who deny him a meaningful structural space visible to themselves. The definee becomes the definer.[16]

Douglass's linguistic dexterity is linked to his need to crystallize the contradictions in Christian America. To gain reader sympathy, he adroitly exploits the ritual impulse embedded in the Christian experience: the heroic soul, victorious over evil, rewarded with life eternal. He therefore superimposes two metaphors—first, the Christian journey, and second, the slave's quest for freedom and literacy. However, it is difficult for slaves to be Christians in this sin-filled world. This finds expression in the spiritual "Lord, I Want to Be a Christian in-a My Heart."[17]

For proof that he preaches the truth, Douglass proceeds to bombard his sympathetic Christian readers with incident upon incident of the "slaveholder's vile corruption, his lust and cruelty, his appetite for unchecked power, his vulgarity and drunkenness, his cowardice, and his damning hypocrisy." Slavery distorts the personality of master and slave. No one is immune, neither the "angelic" Miss Sophia ("Slavery proved as injurious to her as it did to me" [63]), nor his very readers ("We have men-stealers for ministers, women-whippers for missionaries, and cradle-plunderers for church members" [156]). The ultimate reward of slavery for white people, Douglass says, is sin and death of the spirit. This platform enables Douglass, the sermonizer, to appeal to his Christian reader to "come to the abolition movement, and be redeemed."[18]

Finally, perhaps no portrait in Douglass's *Narrative* is as filled with pathos as is the one of his infirm grandmother. She, who had faithfully attended the needs of her master, who "had peopled his plantation with slaves" (76), is unceremoniously sold. Her reward for faithful service is banishment to an isolated cabin in the woods.

16. Baker, *Journey Back,* 31–34.
17. James Weldon Johnson and J. Rosamond Johnson, *The Books of American Negro Spirituals,* 2:72–73.
18. O'Meally, "Frederick Douglass's 1845 *Narrative,*" 197–99.

Douglass's rhetorical flair explodes in the imagination, embroidered with role playing, rhythmical language, and repetition:

> She was nevertheless left a slave—a slave for life—a slave in the hands of strangers; and in their hands she saw her children, her grandchildren, and her great-grandchildren, divided, like so many sheep, without being gratified with the small privilege of a single word. . . . The children, the unconscious children, who once sang and danced in her presence, are gone. She gropes her way, in the darkness of age, for a drink of water. Instead of the voices of her children, she hears by day the moans of the dove, and by night the screams of the hideous owl. All is gloom. The grave is at the door. (76–78)

Douglass, in this heartrending picture of his infirm grandmother, perhaps more so than in any other scene in his *Narrative,* shows the crucial link between the voice of the black preacher as a creator of social values and its sustaining hold on the community of faith.[19] The significance of the black preacher's voice lies in his ability to become the wheel within the wheel as he fills the space within the space and the sound within the sound in order to get inside the unsaid to make the unseen seen. It is in this sense that Douglass's phraseology carries cosmological weight; the ethos of black culture authorizes the black preacher to foster intellectual anarchy—a tradition of protest and resistance—in the face of a morally bankrupt system. That Douglass is acutely aware of the dynamic give and take between preacher and congregation, which drives the suppressed linguistic code and permits the unsaid to enter the community of faith, is indicated by his pauses and stammers:

> My poor old grandmother, the devoted mother of twelve children, is left all alone, in yonder little hut, before a few dim embers. She stands—she sits—she staggers—she falls—she groans—she dies and there are none of her children or grandchildren present, to wipe from her wrinkled brow the cold sweat of death, or to place beneath the sod her fallen remains. Will not a righteous God visit for these things? (78)

19. In his 1855 narrative *My Bondage and My Freedom,* Douglass presents a more nurturing picture of his grandmother. She is held in high esteem by master and slaves (chaps. 1–2). See also Preston, *Young Frederick Douglass.* Preston reminds us that Betsey Bailey, although technically a slave, "neither lived nor behaved like one from 1747 on" (17–21). She died in November 1849.

Moreover, Douglass, in this emotionally charged scene, figuratively lifts the words off the page, as he re-creates the powerful voice of the black preacher, God's trombone. First, Douglass calls his readers to action—end slavery now—and second, he shows the reserves that the black preacher draws upon in his herculean task of keeping his community from dying spiritually. The voice of the black preacher is the indivisible component of the black sermon. Take away the voice of the black preacher and the black sermon ceases to be a culturally unifying document that permits "oppressed African-Americans to create a new world by transcending the narrow confines of the one in which they were forced to live."[20]

To be sure, while Douglass pictures his grandmother as isolated from the community of whites whom she would faithfully have cared for from the cradle to the grave, she is not isolated from her God. What sustains his grandmother (and by implication the slave community) is her ontological comprehension of her relation to God. Through her ritual confrontation with God in her day-to-day activities (praying, singing, sermonizing), his grandmother robs secular confrontations of much of their terror. She thus closes the existential space between God and herself; one might say that she establishes a spiritual comfort zone. For her, religion is not the refuge for the intellectually timid; on the contrary, her daily confrontations with God strengthen her resolve that God will make a way out of no way. In his re-creation of the preacher's voice, Douglass clearly makes the point that prayer and thought are inseparable.

In his detective work *Young Frederick Douglass,* Dickinson Preston, whose purpose is to distinguish between Douglass the man and Douglass the myth, argues persuasively that Douglass engages in poetic liberty in this passage overflowing with emotion. Preston goes to great length to show that Douglass's grandmother, a faithful servant, was not banished to the edge of the plantation. Douglass concedes as much in chapter 2 of *Life and Times.* Instead of seeing it as a false representation of historical facts, though, I suggest that we read this passage as a staging point in the evolution from slave narrative to the early black novel.[21]

20. Levine, *Black Culture,* 33.

21. In "The Heroic Slave," Douglass tried his hand at fiction in his depiction of the Madison Washington mutiny and escape.

The Good That Comes Out of the Black Nazareth

With the question "But who believes any good can come out of the black Nazareth?" in *Iola Leroy,* Frances Ellen Watkins Harper draws attention to the pressures under which the early black novelists labored.[22] These members of a discredited community were driven by twin pressures. First, they were expected to produce a literature that, except for the color of their characters' skin, was a mirror image of the dominant society they aspired to join. Second, they wanted to reaffirm their loyalty to their oppressed community. The former dictated that they not draw attention to differences; the latter demanded that they depict with sympathy the aspirations of black America. In short, they were under tremendous pressure to write novels, as Harper's protagonist mused, that would be a "lasting service for the race" (262).[23] Black Nazareth as metaphor is a contradiction that is both constricting and liberating; it conveys powerlessness and powerfulness.

Implicit in much of nineteenth-century American fiction is the writer's assumption that all citizens enjoy the same freedom of movement to participate in this economic democracy, if only given equal opportunity. The prevailing ideology makes it appear that class power had nothing to do with the inequities of life in America. The American Dream conceals the unimaginable barriers that stand between the typical character and his or her desire (e.g., Huck Finn). Though it exists only subliminally in much of the early black prose fiction, the sermon as a type of repressed black formalism

22. Frances Ellen Watkins Harper, *Iola Leroy* (1987). All citations are to this edition of Harper's novel and are hereafter noted by page numbers in parentheses. For a critique of the conventional pressures that shaped the black novel of the nineteenth century, see Christian, "Uses of History," 165–70. On the oral tradition in black fiction, see Jane Campbell, *Mythic Black Fiction,* 14–15, and James Mellard, "The Popular Mode in Narrative," 6.

23. Arlene Elder, *The "Hindered Hand": Cultural Implications of Early African-American Fiction.* Elder reminds us: "The literary models chosen by nineteenth-century African-American novelists were those of white sentimental and propaganda fiction and, to a lesser degree, Black anti-slavery oratory and autobiographical narrative" (3). Though sublimated, black antislavery oratory (as well as cultural biography) rooted in the church manifests itself in the nearly two dozen novels written by black writers between 1853 and 1910. Also see Bell, *Afro-American Novel.* My interest lies in oratory and the autobiographical impulse, the problematic of sermonic rhetoric, and how the early black prose fiction writers made use of the sermon as a repressed formalism.

challenges these assumptions, as we see when we read fictional representations of black America's "talented tenth" struggling to come to terms with life behind the veil. The writers incorporate sermonic rhetoric in their novels because it provides them with a way of talking about community. The sermonic rhetoric masks much of the emerging class tension in the community.[24]

Reconstruction and post-Reconstruction intensified this class tension, thereby producing a *latent discomfort index* for an emergent black middle class. First, the renewed call for learned ministers created more fragmentation in an already fragmented community. Second, following the Emancipation Proclamation, more blacks joined denominations other than the Baptist and Methodist, such as the Episcopalian, Presbyterian, and Roman Catholic. In practical terms, these middle-class blacks, who set the tone for much of the social and political agenda in the black community, worked diligently to suppress the oral expressive tradition of black people—with the exception of the spirituals—because of its association with the black masses. Determined to be "New Negroes," most middle-class blacks did not want any reminders of their enforced servitude. They were intent on inaugurating a "new order."[25] As a result of cultural ambivalence (and their uncertain position in American society), writers such as Frances Ellen Watkins Harper, Sutton Griggs, Pauline Hopkins, Thomas H. B. Walker, and Paul Laurence Dunbar depicted the black middle class as aspiring toward the mainstream and the lower class as reflecting the folk wisdom of the corporate black community.

These writers' discomfort manifests itself in their uninspired depiction of the complexity of black life. This first generation of African American prose fiction writers were under tremendous pressure to forget as opposed to remembering; that is, they were under a negative pressure not to translate black American oral expressive culture into literary art, especially the oratory of the preacher.[26] They en-

24. Jackson, "Ghetto of the Negro Novel." Jackson reminds us that the early black novel is essentially a middle-class project in terms of its production and orientation. He notes that the early black novelist largely explicates black resourcefulness "in adjusting to a culture aggressively intolerant of [black people]" (183).

25. Alain Locke, "The New Negro," 3–16. In his essay, Locke differentiated the ideological orientation between the "Old Negro" of post-Reconstruction and the militant "New Negro" in the process of this emerging class consciousness that peaked in the 1920s.

26. Harold Bloom, *Agon: Towards a Theory of Revisionism*, 19, and *The Anxiety of*

gaged in a form of aesthetic distancing—the more closely one of their characters approximated Anglo-European sensibilities, the more likely that he or she would mimic the artificial diction of white heroes and heroines. The more refined the character was, the less likely he or she was to be associated with the oral expressive tradition of his or her community.

In her invaluable study *The "Hindered Hand": Cultural Implications of Early African-American Fiction,* Arlene Elder details how the black historic consciousness made its presence felt and rescued these novels from interminable blandness: "Without a doubt, the most important artistic influence of the Black literary tradition on its novelists was as a source of realistic folk characters. Without these believable minor figures, the early novels would bear only a tenuous relationship to the actual lives of Black people in this country."

Furthermore, Elder observes that the major characters in these highly derivative novels "frequently fail to compel belief. . . . Instead, it is with certain minor characters that the humanity of the Black person is salvaged from the fantasy world of popular fiction."[27] Whereas Douglass's *Narrative* in large measure gains its authority from his fidelity to the voice and vision of black America, the majority of the early black novels suffer as a result of their authors' inability to tap into this mythic vision. Consequently, their works lack authority as fictions of power.

For political and cultural reasons, the image of the preacher in the early black novels is either one of a burlesque figure or one of a man beyond reproach. The leadership model of the unlettered black preacher was not only felt to have outlived its usefulness, but many of the writers shied away from re-creating his speech patterns because they saw his language as *prima facie* evidence of the limitations of dialect. In short, they were too self-conscious of the perceived limitations of black speech to lift their collective pens in plumbing the depths of the language for what James Weldon Johnson in a subsequent generation would recognize as their mission to explore "a form that is freer and larger than dialect, but which will still hold the racial flavor . . . which will also be capable of voicing

---

Influence: A Theory of Poetry, 11. I draw here on the vocabulary of Harold Bloom's provocative Freudian theory of poetic influence as the unconscious competitive anxiety in a "strong" poet's ambivalent relationship to his misunderstood predecessor.

27. *"Hindered Hand,"* 52–53.

the deepest and highest emotions and aspirations and allow of the widest range of subjects and the widest scope of treatment," as is evident in Douglass's orchestration of the lines in his vivid description of his grandmother.[28] Behind the design and intention of their narratives lies an unresolved issue: were they Americans who happened to be black or blacks who happened to be Americans? The stance they took dictated their response to black culture, whether the tradition met their political and aesthetic needs.

Writing in another context, Harold Cruse notes that black people will not find the road to liberation under the aegis of mainline white Protestantism in the United States. He counsels that African Americans' political liberation is linked to their drawing spiritual strength from their "black Nazareth." With penetrating insight, Cruse asserts that the historic black church has a role to play in the revitalization of America, provided that it does not fall prostrate before a Eurocentric Christianity:

> As long as the Negro's cultural identity is in question, or open to self-doubts, then there can be no positive identification with the real demands of his political and economic existence. Further than that, without a cultural identity that adequately defines *himself*, the Negro cannot even identify with the American nation as a whole. He is left in the limbo of social marginality, alienated and directionless on the landscape of America.[29]

The religious orientation of black America is at variance with the religion of European immigrants transplanted into American soil. Much of the tension in the fiction of the early black novelists stems from their failure to come to grips with the competing visions of mainline white Protestantism, with its emphasis on a pietistic individualism, and black religion, with its emphasis on "wholeness, reunion, and divine destiny."[30]

The black church makes its presence felt in the fiction of the early black writers in their representation of character, in their tropes of

28. Palosaari, "Image of the Black Minister." See also Daniel, *Images of the Preacher*, and Stephen Henderson, "Worrying the Line: Notes on Black American Poetry," 60–82. Henderson extends the observation that Johnson made in his preface to *The Book of American Negro Poetry* and makes several salient observations on black writers' resistance to and acceptance of the challenge of excavating black speech patterns.

29. *The Crisis of the Negro Intellectual*, 12–13.

30. Gayraud S. Wilmore, Jr., "Black Theology," 93. See also Wilmore and James H. Cone, eds., *Black Theology: A Documentary History, 1966–1979.*

uplift, and in the religious connotation they give to words such as *freedom* and *land* and to themes such as "faith" and "redemption" in America. One concludes that there was tremendous strength of character in the "black Nazareth." Let us briefly examine how Harper and Dunbar incorporate sermonic rhetoric as a type of repressed formalism in their novels.

Of Lasting Service for the Race

Frances Ellen Watkins Harper's *Iola Leroy* is frequently cited as a classic example of the assimilationist novel.[31] Her female protagonist, a paragon of virtue and propriety, embodies protestant virtues. Sheltered from the questionable circumstances of her birth, Harper's heroine is raised as a member of the landed gentry. She learns of her blackness as a shock, prefiguring Du Bois's "double-consciousness."[32]

In *Iola Leroy,* the trope of uplift often overshadows the trope of the "fall." The "fall," as Carby notes, "was used by Harper to indicate the depths of social corruption represented by the institution of slavery; a woman who was socially accepted as white was, within the same society (and text), declared nonhuman and denied all protection and nurturance."[33] Paradoxically, Iola's "fall" precipitates her rise, her strength of character, and the recovery of community that culminates at a small country church, where Iola and her uncle Robert Johnson are reunited with his mother and her grandmother.

Harper introduces her comely heroine to the true nature of black folk religion in a scene that parallels the pythian madness Du Bois recalls in vivid detail in *The Souls of Black Folk:*

31. In this section, I draw upon the work of Hazel Carby, Bernard Bell, Barbara Christian, and Arlene Elder. Harper's text is a prime example of the novel as "counterstereotype" (Elder, *"Hindered Hand,"* 36–66). In "The Uses of History: Frances Harper's *Iola Leroy, Shadows Uplifted,"* Barbara Christian comments on the historical pressures that influenced this literary production. Following the Civil War, Harper, a political activist, tireless lecturer, sentimental poet, and prolific writer, contributed articles to the magazine of the African Methodist Episcopal Church, the *A.M.E. Church Review.* Harper's only novel, *Iola Leroy,* published in Philadelphia in 1892, enjoyed a moderate success. It went quickly into a second printing in 1893 and a third in 1895—it was not reprinted again until 1971. Hazel V. Carby, *Reconstructing Womanhood: The Emergence of the Afro-American Woman Novelist.*

32. *Souls of Black Folk,* 5.

33. Carby, *Reconstructing Womanhood,* 73.

> It was out in the country, far from home, far from my foster home, on a dark Sunday night. The road wandered from our rambling log-house up the stony bed of a creek, past wheat and corn, until we could hear dimly across the fields a rhythmic cadence of song,—soft, thrilling, powerful, that swelled and died sorrowfully in our ears. I was a country school-teacher then, fresh from the East, and had never seen a Southern Negro revival. . . . And so most striking to me, as I approached the village and the little plain church perched aloft, was the air of intense excitement that possessed that mass of black folk. *A sort of suppressed terror hung in the air and seemed to seize us,—a pythian madness, a demoniac possession, that lent terrible reality to song and word. The black and massive form of the preacher swayed and quivered as the words crowded to his lips and flew at us in singular eloquence.*[34]

In her breakthrough reunion, Iola has her first dramatic encounter with the religion of the oppressed. Harper obliquely makes reference to the same kind of phenomena Du Bois described as "pythian madness [and] demoniac possession," which represents the fusion of memory and historical imagination on the part of preacher and community. This fusion of memory and historical imagination shapes the testimony of Robert's mother and gives voice to the scattered community's longing for wholeness:

> "When my little girl," continued the speaker [Robert's mother], "took hole ob dress an' begged me to let her go wid me, an' I couldn't do it, it mos' broke my heart. I had a little boy, an' wen my mistus sole me she kep' him. She carrie on a boardin' house. Many's the time I hab stole out at night an' seen dat chile an' sleep'd wid him in my arms tell mos' day. Bimeby de people I libed wid got hard up fer money, an' I neber laid my eyes on my pore chillen sence den. But, honeys, let de wind blow high or low, I 'spects to outwedder de storm an' anchor by'm bye in bright glory. But I'se bin a prayin' fer one thing, an' I beliebs I'll git it; an' dat is dat I may see my chillen 'fore I die. Pray for medat I may hole out an' hole on, an' neber make a shipwreck ob faith, an' at las' fine my way from earth to glory" (181).

The bonding that takes place in and during this ritual of community frees the normally concealed public memory. (The community erupts in "a paroxysm of joy" [182] when Robert responds to his mother's call on the Lord to see her children before she dies.) From

34. *Souls of Black Folk,* 155 (emphasis added).

the standpoint of a community oppressed in history, this guarded public memory reveals "a critique of community and a fascination with the possibility and hope of intimacy."[35] As a representation of desire, it reveals a world in which those oppressed in history will no longer exist as racialized subjects. As a community, the people are free to make private memory public (the "suppressed terror") and to affirm their essential humanity (the "massive form of the preacher [that] swayed and quivered"), which exists prior to and beyond the ideology of oppression.

Although the preacher is absent from the testimonials given by those who are in search of loved ones at the church conference that Iola attends, his presence is felt in their autobiographical recollections full of pathos. Their religious worldview represents their attempt to come to terms with the radicality of the American experience even as they struggle to find a voice that will articulate their vision. They are in fact engaged in an ongoing search for community in America. Fathers and mothers passionately tell of their desire to be reunited with members of their scattered families and testify as to how their faith has sustained them in the midnight of their despair. The genesis of the spiritual vision has origin in these cries straight from the heart.

In telling of his search for his mother, the handsome Robert, who could easily be these fathers' and mothers' son, validates their call for community. His mother's rapturous response authenticates the community's faith. Among this group who are her social inferiors, Iola first experiences and participates in the community of the oppressed.[36] Suggestive of the "demonic dread" the supplicant experiences in the presence of the divine, the group ethos that informs the folk religion conflicts with the Protestant individualism that Iola embodies.

The reunion scene represents an early manifestation in black American literature of the folk religious spirit that binds blacks in a way they are not bound to other Americans because of their different histories. This emotion-filled scene is as close as Harper comes to the radicality of the experience of blacks in America. These rural black folk are separated by a "vast and physical and metaphorical

35. Long, *Significations,* 165–66.
36. Ibid., 158–72, 181–83.

distance" from those intellectuals who represent the race at the "conversazione" in chapter 30, "Friends of the Council." In *Reconstructing Womanhood,* Carby argues persuasively that Harper represents "'the people' [whom Iola and Robert encounter in their search for family] as metaphorical 'folk,' which in its rural connotations avoided and ignored the implication of the presence of black city workers," or, in this instance, the emergence of a black intellectual class.[37]

The reunion scene further buttresses Iola Leroy's desire to be of service to the race, which prefigures the narrator's desire in *The Autobiography of an Ex-Coloured Man* "to be a great coloured man."[38] Iola's desire to be a great woman in a society that sees her first as a black woman is given expression by the talented tenth in the chapters that conclude the novel. The group is a metaphorical figuration on the part of certain segments in the black community to transcend race. We see the emergence of competing class interests wherein the religious imagination that had been preoccupied with land and dignity yields before assimilation and elitism. There was a subtle but perceptible shift in the religious address of the community with the large-scale movement of black people to the cities of the industrial North in the early decades of the twentieth century.

The Sport of the Gods

In *The Sport of the Gods,* Paul Laurence Dunbar provides us with a genesis of a new form hammered into being on the anvil of the black body.[39] He does not do ritualistic obeisance to what I shall call "uplift fundamentalism," with its attendant evangelical fervor. He provides us with the first literary representation of a painstaking exegesis of the tortuous journey of blacks from peasants to denizens of the urban metropolis. In the process, he provides us with an alternate reading of the American Dream.

Religion in *The Sport of the Gods* has little of the mystical and metaphysical import that it has in Harper's *Iola Leroy* or Sutton Griggs's *Imperium in Imperio* (1889). Ohio native Dunbar breaks with

37. *Reconstructing Womanhood,* 164–65. See also Carby, "Ideologies of Black Folk: The Historical Novel of Slavery," 125–43.

38. Johnson, *Autobiography of an Ex-Coloured Man,* 46.

39. *The Sport of the Gods* (1970). All citations are to this edition of Dunbar's novel and are hereafter noted by page numbers in parentheses.

a whole cast of thought (that is generously supported by American and African American tradition) wherein preaching is still the highest boon open to the religious imagination.

The social transformation that Dunbar outlines—the social consciousness required for suffering in the urban metropolis—expresses itself in the blues and the gospel sound. And in Dunbar's literary production, the victory goes to the defiant sister, hardened by her years in New York, who emerges as a blues figure. A fragmented community must evolve gods to keep pace with its rapid social transformation. The blues aesthetic that dominates Dunbar's hymn to urbanization represents the inability of traditional religion to meet the needs of a peasant people struggling to adapt in an alien world of industrial clock time.

Set in the American South during Reconstruction, *The Sport of the Gods* is a tale of two families, with the black family mirroring the values of the white family. After many years of faithful service to the white Benson family, Berry Hamilton, the father of the black family, is falsely accused of stealing. When he is sentenced to a long jail term, his once respectable family, disgraced, migrates to New York and slowly disintegrates. After five years in jail, Berry is released, thanks to the hard work of a newspaper reporter. By this time, his son is in jail for murder, his daughter is a blues singer, and his wife has taken up with another man. The Hamiltons do not so much repudiate a way of life as embrace one that is alien to their system of values because they are forced to.

During their descent into immorality (the fall from innocence into experience), the Hamilton children call into question the promise of America and the real meaning of human kindness, as is evident in Sadness's monologue to a disoriented Joe Hamilton: "You see, Hamilton, in this life we are all suffering from fever, and no one edges away from the other because he finds him a little warm. It's dangerous when you're not used to it; but once you go through the parching process, you become inoculated against further contagion" (114).

Sadness, the eternal parasite, speaks the language of the dispossessed urban proletariat, who realize the cruel joke that has been played on them when they discover themselves prisoners in the city of refuge. The novel concludes with a dispirited Berry and his wife returning to the South in hopes of beginning life anew.

Dunbar does not give a ringing endorsement to the notion that success and material goods are to be found in the city. His midwestern agrarian values coincided at many points with the anti-industrial bias for the plantation tradition. James Weldon Johnson and Zora Neale Hurston were among the first to recognize the disappearance of peasant culture. They had enough emotional distance from the experience of black enslavement to recognize the value of preservation of oral expressive cultural forms. The image of the city that Dunbar sketches in a broad outline culminates in Richard Wright's classic critique of the urban nightmare in *Native Son.*

For Dunbar, the breakup of a feudal society signals the fact that the language of religion has lost its effectiveness as the glue that holds this static world together. The preacher derives much of his power through the myth of religion, which is itself dependent on the fallacy of sin. From the African American perspective, this myth is conditioned on the erroneous premise that blackness is a sign of inferiority. Many in the Euro-American religious fraternity have had great difficulty in coming to grips with a theology of concealment premised on the mistaken notion that black skin is a sign of evil.

The club competes aggressively with the church as the focal point of ritual space. Dunbar shows us that many lower-class black migrants create religious substitutes in this secular space that are as consuming for them as is the church for many of their mainstream brothers and sisters. Hence, there is no compelling reason for him to provide the reader with a positive representation of the preacher.[40] It is for this reason that Dunbar breaks with the tradition of slave narrative as a rhetorical device through which black slaves articulated their humanity in the search for freedom from physical and psychological bondage. Zora Neale Hurston recovers this impulse in *Their Eyes Were Watching God.*

Most of the nineteenth-century black writers created a textual

40. Kate Millet, *Sexual Politics.* This in part explains Dunbar's uncomplimentary picture of the preacher in his "raceless" novel *The Uncalled,* which is frequently read as autobiographical, as it tells the story of a young man who is trying to decide whether to become a minister. At one time Dunbar struggled with the idea of becoming a minister. Millet sees an even more vicious corollary in sexual caste, which "supersedes all other forms of inegalitarianism: racial, political, or economic" (20).

experience that muted the nationalistic impulses of the community; their narratives promoted assimilationist aesthetics and tended to marginalize black oral culture. Paradoxically, their characters' futile attempts to escape out of history drove them to confront the bloody history of their slave past. Their consciousness of their slave past was closely linked to the issues of defining self and finding a voice to articulate that self. To resolve contradictions, these writers often drew on the rhetoric of the black preacher to resolve conflicts about race and rights—conflicts that remain with us today.

3

Recontextualizing the Sermon to Tell (Her)story

Their Eyes Were Watching God

Zora Neale Hurston wrote in *Their Eyes Were Watching God* from the interiority of black culture. The fact that she saw religion as a mode of making sense of the experiences of a black tradition makes *Their Eyes Were Watching God* a strong, assertive statement. In contrast, many of the novels of the 1920s and 1930s view blackness as a pathology. Carl Van Vechten's *Nigger Heaven* and Claude McKay's *Home to Harlem,* for example, emphasize the exotic primitive, while Jesse Fauset's *There Is Confusion* and Nella Larsen's *Passing* emphasize assimilation. For this reason, *Their Eyes Were Watching God,* along with Hurston's work as an anthropologist and folklorist, bears witness to the desire of black people to argue, live, love, and die in a place of their own creation and to center themselves in a universe independent of the tyranny of man-made states of oppression. That she set her novel of romantic love in Eatonville, Florida, one of the first all-black towns in the United States, is itself a religious expression. Hurston thus challenged black writers to enter the mainstream of American society on their own terms, which means to accept and promote the integrity of black culture. To the extent that she externalized through language the values of black culture, Hurston saved the text.

Hurston's power in *Their Eyes Were Watching God* centers on her ability to fix the cultural values in language and in the work of art;

these values are artistic form. Like the preacher, Hurston's artistic gift "consists in discovering the not-yet-discovered subsistent values and meanings that make up [her text]'s object in the creative act which is the revelation of that object in and through the language."[1] In other words, *Their Eyes Were Watching God* brings the values and meanings of the culture to its participants' attention. The narrative performs a normative function; the participants espouse the values and meanings that the narrative reveals.

The end product of Hurston's vision is the creation of a new black woman through a critique of the past. In looking back, Janie also looks forward to the day when American women of African descent will no longer be the mules of the world. Using familiar Bible-based tropes and metaphors, Hurston drives to the heart of a series of related questions: What does it mean to be black and female in America? What are the terms of definition for women outside the traditional hierarchies? Is female status negated without a male defining principle? And she raises these questions to reveal to the black community the one face it can never see: its own.

Although Hurston's narrative orientation focuses on the emergence of a female self in a male-dominated world, she tells her magnificent story of romantic love against the background of church and extrachurch modes of expression. Understanding this fact helps to explain those sections of the narrative that have been said to have no meaning beyond their "entertainment" value, such as the joking on the front porch of Joe Starks's store about Matt Bonner's mule.[2] Hurston knew that the religious life of Americans of African descent manifested itself in all spheres of life. The extrachurch modes of expression possess great critical and creative powers that have often touched religious issues regarding the true situation of black communities that are deeper than those of the institutional black church. These church and extrachurch modes of expression may be seen in the narrative structure, in the texture of language and imagery, and in the manner in which language itself is alive with history and historical struggle in the telling of the emergence of a female self in a male-dominated world.

Divided into three sections that correspond roughly to modes of

1. Eliseo Vivas, "The Object of the Poem," 1074.
2. Robert E. Hemenway, *Zora Neale Hurston: A Literary Biography*, 218.

religious expression, *Their Eyes Were Watching God* celebrates the art of the community, a celebration presented in such a manner that "the harsh edges of life in a Jim Crow South seldom come into view."[3] Section 1 has a spiritual orientation and covers the time of Janie's marriage to Logan Killacks (which sets in motion the initial tension in the novel—that between Janie and her grandmother over what a woman ought to be and do); section 2 focuses on the richness and diversity of the styles of life in the black community (black people's will to adorn and their sense of drama daily are put on display on Joe Starks's storefront porch); and section 3, which focuses on the blues impulse, covers Janie's life with Tea Cake in the Everglades (and provides movement toward the resolution of the tension that has sent Janie to the horizon and back). Given Janie's history, an overarching question that unifies these sections is: what rescues Janie from becoming a full-fledged blues figure? And one might also ask whether Hurston is ambivalent about this.

Their Eyes Were Watching God is a story within a story, deeply influenced by the power of language and myth in and out of the homiletical mode. The received language "dictates" that *Their Eyes Were Watching God,* though set in Florida, must occur outside of a specific time and place. (This requirement receives its fullest deployment in James Baldwin's *Go Tell It on the Mountain.*) By placing her narrative in the context of the Christian journey, itself a romance, Hurston overrides reader expectation that the protagonist should marry her black Prince Charming and live happily ever after. Having returned from the horizon, Janie Woods represents the mature voice of experience and wisdom as she retrospectively tells her story to one who is, from an experiential point of view, a novice. Janie intends to convert Pheoby, and Hurston intends to convert the reader-participant. Her first move in her conversion narrative is to revise the patriarchal convention of seeing the world through a male dialectic.

Janie's story, as sermon and as testimony, merges the material with the spiritual world. This constitutes the "unsaid" in the novel's arrestingly powerful opening scene:

> Ships at a distance have every man's wish on board. For some they come in with the tide. For others they sail forever on the

3. Ibid.

> horizon, never out of sight, never landing until the Watcher turns his eyes away in resignation, his dreams mocked to death by Time. That is the life of men.
>
> Now, women forget all those things they don't want to remember, and remember everything they don't want to forget. The dream is the truth. Then they act and do things accordingly.[4]

Hurston presents us with the classical biblical picture of the looker standing before the horizon and wondering if she and the horizon shall ever meet. The looker sees a picture that is both in time and timeless, finite and infinite. The ships on the horizon are emblematic of the dreams of the person standing on the shore. This timeless picture speaks of a person's life to be related to God, the ultimate Other, "a need in the moment of existence to belong, to be related to a beginning and to an end."[5]

As her story unfolds, we come to realize that the naive sixteen-year-old Janie, as the looker, stands before the horizon (the pear tree in bloom) as one whose spiritual loyalties are "completely divided, as [is], without question, her mind."[6] Her spiritual loyalties are divided because she has not yet earned the unspeakable intimacy that bonds the community of faith. In contrast to her grandmother, Janie lacks the faith-knowledge that comes from a firsthand experience with the Holy Spirit.

Faith-knowledge does not rely on the evidence of the senses but is, in the scriptural phrase, "the evidence of things not seen"—that is, not presented to sense perception—and it would lose its essential nature and be transformed into a mere sorry empirical knowledge if it relied on any other evidence than "the witness of the Holy Spirit," which is not that of sense experience.[7]

Sustained by her faith-knowledge born in the midnight of despair of the slave experience, Nanny, a recognizable figure in the black community, breaks the pervasive silence of her sixteen-year "silent worship" as she passionately tells Janie of her dream. Her sermonic monologue, one of the most moving scenes in all of black

4. *Their Eyes Were Watching God*, 1. All citations are from the 1990 edition and are hereafter noted by page numbers in parentheses.

5. Frank Kermode, *The Sense of an Ending*, 4.

6. Alice Walker, *In Search of Our Mother's Garden*, 236.

7. Rudolf Otto, *The Idea of the Holy*, 228.

American literature, serves to order experience. Janie's life is the sermon, as Nanny makes clear:

> Ah wanted to preach a great sermon about colored women sittin' on high, but they wasn't no pulpit for me. Freedom found me wid a baby daughter in mah arms, so *on my knees* Ah said *to my God* Ah'd take a broom and a cook-pot and throw up a highway through de wilderness for her. She would expound what Ah felt. But somehow she got lost offa de highway and next thing Ah knowed here you was in de world. So whilst Ah was tendin' you of nights Ah said Ah'd save de text for you. (emphasis added; 15–16)

The text that Nanny saves is the cultural genealogy of black America in general and of the black woman in particular. This believable, manageable fiction centers on an interpretation of history that is consistent with a Judeo-Christian view that emphasizes patience, humility, and good nature. Created by blacks in the face of limited options, this interpretation of history makes it possible for many in the oppressed corporate community to interpret their behavior as being Christlike. In fact, the posture adopted by Nanny is necessary for the maintenance of self-esteem rather than as the realization of the Christian ideal. With each of her three marriages, Janie challenges this externally imposed stereotype, which served in slavery as the ideal self-image for the corporate community.[8]

Janie's application of the text, her reinterpretation of history, provides her with the impetus to break free of gendered silence and inferior status. In her movement from passive looker to active participant, Janie discovers that in order to change one's way of thinking, the individual must change her perceptions of the world. Whereas Nanny and Janie share the same mythic belief system, they differ in their means to reach the goal, the dream.

In many respects, the tension to be resolved in the Nanny-Janie argument involves the route to freedom and respectability for the black woman. This is presented in the novel as two competing perspectives on reality: Janie's romantic vision and Nanny's pragmatic grounding in reality. They have different interpretations and applications of the dream of "whut a woman oughta be and to do" (15), which is to say, they have different interpretations of history. Whereas Nanny, whose brooding presence dominates the narrative,

8. S. P. Fullinwider, *The Mind and Mood of Black America*, 27–28.

sees the dream as protection and security, Janie sees Nanny's dream as restrictive; it circumscribes existence. The grandmother's dream has no room for an idyllic view of nature. For Nanny the pressure of history is a pressure in favor of remembering and not forgetting, whereas for Janie the pressure of history is in favor of forgetting and against remembering.[9]

The tension between Nanny and Janie as presented in the opening paragraphs centers on the highly charged word *truth,* meaning 'to be free from other people's fictions.' What is the truth as socially constructed: security and respect (Logan Killacks), excessive competition and overcompensation as a result of marginalization (Joe Starks), or the sensualization of pain and pleasure (Tea Cake and life on the Everglades)? These versions of the truth, presented from the perspective of black males, confront the female looker as she stands before the horizon: "Now, women forget all those things they don't want to remember, and remember everything they don't want to forget. The dream is the truth. Then they act and do things accordingly."

This enigmatic opening begins to make sense in the wake of Jody's death, when Janie allows her suppressed emotions to surface: "She had an inside and an outside now and suddenly she knew how not to mix them" (68). Janie has come to an awareness of the fact that her grandmother has pointed her in the wrong direction—a realization that her grandmother's best of intentions had contributed to her divided self:

> She had been getting ready for her great journey to the horizons in search of *people;* it was important to all the world that she should find them and they find her. But she had been whipped like a cur dog, and run off down a back road after *things.* It was all according to the way you see things. Some people could look at a mud-puddle and see an ocean with ships. But Nanny belonged to that other kind that loved to deal in scraps. Here Nanny had taken the biggest thing God ever made, the horizon—for no matter how far a person can go the horizon is still way beyond you—and pinched it in to such a little bit of a thing that she could tie it about her granddaughter's neck tight enough to choke her. (85)

In the wake of this realization, Janie begins earnestly the process of her search for self and form, the process of finding a voice and

9. Stanley E. Fish, *Self-Consuming Artifacts,* 6.

creating a woman. The process of healing her divided mind includes rejecting protection and security, which Nanny, Logan, and Jody sought to provide, and entering into a relationship with a man regarded as her social inferior. Coming to see the world created by her grandmother's well-intended actions as a fiction, Janie, in her search for self and form, turns her world upside down in order to make it right-side up. The break from gendered silence—exemplified by the negative community of gossiping women who sit on the front porch—involves the reconnection of subject (Janie) and object (pear tree) on the same imaginative plane; that is, Janie in her quest unknowingly sets out to smash a fiction that has outlived its usefulness: black women as the mules of the world.

The polarity represented by Nanny in her concentration on security and Janie in her movement toward the horizon stems from Janie's desire to seek an authentic place for an expression of the autonomy and independence of her consciousness. Janie's desire is similar to that embedded in the ethos and telos of black religion:

> The desire for an authentic place for the expression of this reality is the source of the revolutionary tendencies in [black religion]. But on the level of human consciousness, religions of the oppressed create in another manner. The hegemony of the oppressors is understood as a myth—a myth in the two major senses, as true and as fictive. It is true as a structure with which one must deal in a day-to-day manner if one is to persevere, but it is fictive as far as any ontological significance is concerned.[10]

It is in their day-to-day existence as laborers that members of the oppressed community challenge the oppressors' definition of them. Their autonomy arises from their labor; paradoxically, their own autonomy takes on a fictive character. The principal figures in Janie's life respond to the contradictory nature of myth as true in a variety of ways. Nanny's intimate knowledge of the violence perpetuated upon the corporate community dictates her determination to have her granddaughter marry in order to protect her from such a history. Joe Starks's response to history is to overcompensate by lording his accomplishments over his fellow citizens. Tea Cake's response is to seek freedom and release through his music and style of life; the perpetual mobility of this blues figure is indicative of his

10. Long, *Significations,* 169–70.

not becoming "institutionally" dependent on a system over which he exercises no control. Tea Cake remains outside the system. Though the blues as a "religious" counterstatement against the fictive character of the corporate community's autonomy stand outside the sway of the institutional church, the community of faith (Nanny) understands its anarchic personality. In her movement toward the horizon, the sheltered Janie will come to understand the fugitive element that makes the music swing, jump, cry.

Crayon Enlargements

In the Eatonville section, Hurston focuses on the style of life in a vibrant and dynamic community. From her perspective, best-foot-forward presentations of the folk represent the triumph of the human spirit over oppression, meaning that black enjoyment of life "is not solely a product of defensive *re*actions" to the dominant white culture. Hurston believed that the distinguishing feature, the corporate signature, of the African imagination in America is creativity—the ability to invest the Other's linguistic structure with new meanings. In "Characteristics of Negro Expression," she referred to this irrepressible quality as "the will to adorn." That which permeates the soul of the black community is drama. Hurston commented: "Every phase of Negro life is highly dramatized. No matter how joyful or how sad the case there is sufficient poise for drama. Everything is acted out. Unconsciously for the most part of course. There is an impromptu ceremony always ready for every hour of life. No little moment passes unadorned." Hurston implicitly presents blacks as offering an image of vitality in a civilization dimly aware of its lack of both vitality and color.[11]

In terms of narrative tension, Hurston contrasts this vitality with the increasingly withdrawn Janie, who is excluded from participating in the storytelling sessions, the "crayon enlargements of life" (48) on the storefront porch. She has become a prisoner of the pretty picture of "whut a woman oughta be and to do," as outlined by Joe when he courted her: "A pretty doll-baby lak you is made to sit on de front porch and rock and fan yo'self and eat p'taters dat other folks plant just special for you" (28).

11. Hemenway, *Zora Neale Hurston*, 221, and Hurston, *Sanctified Church*, 50, 49; see also Carby, "Ideologies of Black Folk," 125–43. Bennett, *Negro Mood*, 49.

The imaginative freedom that the big-picture talkers have on the front porch contrasts with Janie's despair inside the store, where she silently listens with the dumb obedience of a mule. Forced to become a passive observer, Janie longs to participate in these spirited storytelling sessions, the male community in unison enjoying release from the day's work. "Janie loved the conversation and sometimes she thought up good stories on the mule, but Joe had forbidden her to indulge" (50). The restricted space gnaws away at her soul. Squeezed out of the big picture, an appendage who derives her identity through her husband, Mrs. Mayor Starks finds herself ensnared in a choking kind of love; this is not what she had envisioned under the pear tree.

Reserved for the big-picture talkers, the porch of Joe Starks's store is treated as a sacred space wherein secular performances take place. Within this space, the storytellers exhibit the creative capacities of black people defining themselves in the order of things. Like their preacher counterparts, the personae the storytellers employ in performance sanction these men as guardians of the word, of the text—of the aesthetic values of the community. The performance, with its dynamic give-and-take that one associates with the black church, runs through all segments of black life.

Matt Bonner's decrepit mule is the focal point of the daily drama played out in the ritual space of Joe's storefront porch. Sam and Lige and Walter take the lead in creating the "pictures" the male members pass around, which an envious Janie rightly divines as "crayon enlargements of life":

> "Dat mule uh yourn, Matt. You better go see 'bout him. He's bad off."
>
> "Where 'bouts? Did he wade in de lake and uh alligator ketch him?"
>
> "Worser'n dat. De womenfolks got yo' mule. When Ah come round de lake 'bout noontime mah wife and some others had 'im flat on de ground usin' his sides fuh uh wash board."
>
> The great clap of laughter that they have been holding in, bursts out. Sam never cracks a smile. "Yeah, Matt, dat mule so skinny till de women is usin' his rib bones fun uh rub-board, and hangin' things out on his hock-bones tuh dry." (49)

These good-natured stories show that the creative capacities of blacks are not dependent on living in trembling and fear of the white man—nor do the tales use white oppression as a point of departure. Coexisting with the laughter, banter, and humor of the jokes about Matt Bonner's mule are references to the poverty and marginality, as well as the life-and-death struggle for survival, especially when the buzzards swoop down to eat the dead mule. The humor, however, takes the edge off the tale-tellers' poverty and their marginality (the sides of the mule are so flat as to be used as washboards).

The stories told on Joe Starks's porch appear to have significance beyond their immediate entertainment value. The people who make fun of Matt Bonner's tired mule can identify with this beast of burden, which works in dumb obedience and silence much as they have been trained—and more, *pronounced*—to do, and as Joe has trained Janie to do. But unlike the mule, she rebels rather than going silently to her grave.

Imagistically, the humor inherent in the mock funeral for the mule may be read on two levels. First, the parody of mule heaven crystallizes the people's desire for a better world—plenty of food and no work. Second, it echoes Nanny's desire not to have Janie work with little or no tangible rewards for herself. The frustrated Janie is isolated from the imaginative life of the community; she cannot texturize the world.

Overall the stories in this section are not so much documents for understanding black life as they are representations of Hurston's attempt to capture the vibrancy and drama that are part of the creative soul of black America. As Hemenway notes, Hurston's efforts "were intended to show rather than tell, the assumption being that both behavior and art will become self-evident as the tale texts and hoodoo rituals accrete during the reading."[12]

To know how a people view the world around them is to understand how they evaluate life; and a people's temporal and nontemporal evaluations of life provide them with a charter of action, a guide to behavior. In this regard, Hurston makes it explicit that Christian explanations have never proved fully adequate for blacks, whose sensibilities are deeply rooted in the folk traditions. In chapter 8, for example, the reader is more inclined to rejoice in Janie's confronting Joe on his deathbed about the woman she has become—

12. Hemenway, *Zora Neale Hurston*, 168.

declaring her independence—than to note the extent to which extrachurch forms of expression (remnants of African traditional religion) inform this pivotal scene. Hurston, in a statement radical for its time, brings to the surface these submerged values, beliefs, and practices in her depiction of the root doctor and in Janie's description of Joe's death. Though Hurston does not give an exegetical explanation of the religious values that underlie Joe's calling on the root doctor, she makes it clear that his apparent act of desperation is interrelated with Janie's description of her husband's death. In making these extrachurch forms of expression central to our understanding of Joe and Janie Starks, the town's most venerated citizens, Hurston perceptively reveals the epic complexity of black life.

As he nears death, the status-conscious Joe engages the assistance of a conjure man to ward off the spell he believes Janie, his wife of twenty years, has had put on him. Hurston suggests that although African traditional religion and medicine, which the root doctor represents, have been forced underground, these once viable traditional values and outlooks continue to exist and to exercise an influence among segments of the corporate community, as Pheoby indicates in her all-knowing, sympathetic response to the shocked Janie: "Janie, Ah thought maybe de thing would die down and you never would know nothin' 'bout it, but it's been singin' round here ever since de big fuss in de store dat Joe was 'fixed' and you wuz de one dat did it" (78).

As a representative of a once proud living tradition, the root doctor has been forced underground and divested of an essential dimension of his raison d'être. Known in Africa as medicine men, herbalists, traditional doctors, or *wangangas,* and also knowledgeable in religious matters, these influential African men and women are expected "to be trustworthy, upright morally, friendly, willing and ready to serve, able to discern people's needs and not be exorbitant in their charges." But in the face of an uncompromising and indifferent Christianity, Hurston's root doctor, as a remnant of African traditional religion and medicine on the North American continent, is forced to stand outside the dominant Christian culture as something foreign and alien. The root doctor in America, as the public face of a submerged religion, is reduced to a caricature of his or her former self. Operating at the edge of American society, the root doctor is more likely to be a charlatan or a hustler than "the friend of the community [who] comes into the picture at many points in individual and community life."[13]

Hurston demonstrates her understanding of the complexity of the black experience, with its discontinuity within continuity, in the stressful departure scene between Joe and Janie. That this scene is filled with subtle juxtaposition of thought and idea becomes apparent when Janie thinks of death:

> Death, that strange being with the huge square toes who lived way in the West. The great one who lived in the straight house like a platform without sides to it and without a roof. What need has Death for a cover, and what winds can blow against him? He stands in his high house that overlooks the world. Stands watchful and motionless all day with his sword drawn back, waiting for the messenger to bid him come. Been standing there before there was a where or a when or a then. (79–80)

Janie's conception of death reveals the manner in which language itself is alive with history and the historical to tell of the emergence of a black ethos in an Eurocentric world. Like her African American ancestors before her, Janie uses the language and imagery of the Christian Bible because it is readily available. Nevertheless, her aesthetic orientation differs from those in the dominant community, as is evident in her conceptualization of death. Hurston presents a well-developed religious consciousness that has penetrated the universe in ways the dominant culture has not. For example, in her attitude toward death and dying, Janie displays a certain intimacy. Her conceptualization stands in sharp contrast to the conventional Western attitude toward death. Death is not final; God has not died in Africa. Physical death is a passage from one realm of existence to another. As long as there is God, man or woman will never be a *finite* being.

In conjoining the mainstream Janie with the root doctor, Hurston adds an encyclopedic sweep to her novel. She illuminates how a submerged cultural formation acts upon and mediates the construction of a self. While one might argue that, as a matter of historical genesis, the association might have been awakened in Janie's mind during a moment of stress, the inward and lasting

13. John S. Mbiti, *African Religions and Philosophy,* 1–2.

character of these interlocking passages is to make the connection that, in the United States, the root doctor has become separated from his divine calling. Hurston would have us understand that African traditional medicine is a part of African traditional religion.[14]

What Hurston, in effect, is evoking is the historical genesis of the blues—the reconstitution of self out of a religion that is viewed as foreign and alien. She is talking about black people's ability to squeeze out a song, story, or sermon from the near-lyric, near-tragic situation of their lives in spite of their inability to texturize the world.[15] Ultimately, the text for Hurston is not a fixed object but a dialectical process in which contradictory elements coexist, in which parts and wholes depend upon each other, and in which negation and affirmation are closely joined. It is in this sense that we can speak of Hurston as showing how an African continuum is maintained. In spite of the fragmentation that has occurred, the corporate community maintains continuity in the face of discontinuity and discontinuity in the face of continuity.

The Blues Impulse

If Hurston's intent in the first two sections of *Their Eyes Were Watching God* is to screen out white antipathy, then the last section shows the response of the community to white oppression and its assignment of marginality to the black community. Hurston does not view the blues as the failure of religion, but as the intensification of religious expression in the absence of fundamental checks and balances of the strong against the weak. While the perpetrators of the oppression remain essentially in the background, the effects of their oppression manifest themselves in the hedonistic lifestyles of many in the black community. Not surprisingly, Janie discovers her voice among the socially downcast segment of society, those who sensualize pain and pleasure. After twenty years of marriage, Jody dies and Janie falls in love with Vergible "Tea Cake" Woods, a man twelve years younger than she and, by most people's estimations, her social

14. Mbiti, *African Religions*, 217–52, and Shorter, *African Christian Theology*, 1–19. I have written at greater length about Voodoo as a submerged religion in an article entitled "Society and Self in Alice Walker's *In Love and Trouble*," *Obsidian II* 6, no. 2 (Summer 1991): 50–75.

15. Ralph Ellison, *Shadow and Act*, 250.

inferior. In a reversal of the romantic moment that we associate with fairy tales such as the Cinderella story, Janie and Tea Cake go to live in the Everglades, rejecting the finery and status of the mayor's house because of their desire to know and love each other.

Janie's life with Tea Cake, a cultural archetype, represents her third and final movement in her march toward the horizon, toward self-definition. Tea Cake, as the blues-made-flesh, is the objectification of Janie's desire. In spite of his sexism, Tea Cake, a rounder, drifter, day laborer, is the embodiment of the freedom that Janie's divided mind has long sought. And unlike the traditional bluesman, Tea Cake does not love Janie and then leave her.

Tea Cake's lifestyle expresses a practical, existential response to the world and stands in direct opposition to the values Nanny had attempted to instill in Janie. A hedonistic howl replaces silent worship; the desire for security and stability yields to comfort with flux. Whereas Nanny's life was dedicated to the patient forbearance of Christian Protestant worship, Tea Cake's life—with its roots in the slave seculars—represents another dimension of the day-to-day secular expression of the community. Tea Cake's irrepressible laughter embodies the tough-minded spirit of the blues. It stands as a reminder that there had to be more to the everyday than the struggle for material subsistence.

The tradition that Tea Cake embodies recognizes no dichotomy between a spiritual and a blues mystique. The blues are the spirituals, good is bad, God is the devil, and every day is Saturday. The essence of the tradition is the extraordinary tension between the poles of pain and joy, agony and ecstasy, good and bad, Sunday and Saturday. Unlike the spiritual vision, the blues vision "deals with a world where the inability to solve a problem does not necessarily mean that one can, or ought, to transcend it."[16] Tea Cake, who stands outside the influence of the institutional church, responds to his circumscribed existence by squeezing as much pleasure out of the moment as possible. Needless to say, his lifestyle, in contrast to Nanny's patient forbearance, is tantamount to paganism.

Tea Cake, who appears to live only for the moment, comes from "an environment filled with heroic violence, flashing knives, Satur-

16. Bennett, *Negro Mood,* 50. See also Sherly Anne Williams, "The Blues Roots of Contemporary Afro-American Poetry," 74–75.

day night liquor fights, and the magnificent turbulence of a blues-filled weekend of pleasure and joy."[17] This child of the morning star makes Janie feel alive, vital, needed, loved, unlimited—and she gives of herself freely. Janie's blissful "marriage" with Tea Cake lasts for about two years; then a storm hits the Everglades, and God takes His glance away.

During the raging storm, God seems to be speaking. Janie and Tea Cake wait on God to make His move, and when destruction seems imminent, Janie and Tea Cake strike out for the high ground. In a heroic struggle against the raw power of nature, they make it, but not before Tea Cake is bitten by a rabid dog in an effort to save Janie. Several weeks later, Janie is forced to kill the man she loves. As "a glance from God" (102), Tea Cake has been temporary. "The Lord giveth, and the Lord taketh away."[18]

Janie's response to the flood is not simply intellectual; it is experiential and total. It is a religious response born out of her having come to terms with the impenetrable majesty of the divine. For Janie, the experience of *mysterium tremendum* is brought to bear when she is suspended between life and death:

> "If you kin see de light at daybreak, you don't keer if you die at dusk. It's so many people never seen de light at all. Ah wuz fumblin' round and God opened de door."
>
> The wind came back with triple fury, and put out the light for the last time. They sat in company with the others in other shanties, their eyes straining against crude walls and their souls asking if He meant to measure their puny might against His. They seemed to be staring at the dark, but their eyes were watching God. (151)

The storm in this, Janie's last movement toward the horizon, symbolizes the struggle of the corporate black community to come to terms with the oppressor's negation of its image. Out of this negation, the mythic consciousness seeks a *new* beginning in the future by imagining an *original* beginning. The social implications of this religious experience enable the oppressed community to dehistoricize the oppressor's hegemonic dominance. Metaphorically, the phrase *their eyes were watching God* means they were watching the creation of a new form of humanity—one that is no longer based

17. Barksdale, "Margaret Walker," 110–11.
18. Lillie P. Howard, *Zora Neale Hurston*, 105–6.

on the master-slave dialectic. The utopian and eschatological dimensions of the religions of the oppressed stem from this modality—which Hurston arrests by concluding her moving story of romantic love with a flourish of Christian iconography.

With the spellbound Pheoby at her side, Janie struggles to find her voice and, equally important, an audience that will give assent to her testimony. Janie taps into the responsive mythology of the black sermon as she assigns meaning to her experience. She exercises autonomy in making her world through language. However, while the language of the black church provides her one means of translating Janie's experience into a medium that can be comprehended easily by a member of her aesthetic community, Hurston keeps before us the inescapable fact that the community acts upon Janie, and Janie upon the community. She differs from her community in that her action is a break from gendered silence.

The logical conclusion to Janie's female-centered discourse occurs when Pheoby, who aspires "to sit on de front porch" (28), undergoes a transformation. With the exhilaration that only the newly converted can know, Pheoby enthusiastically becomes Janie's disciple: "Lawd!" Pheoby breathed out heavily, "Ah done growed ten feet higher from jus' listenin' tuh you, Janie. Ah ain't satisfied wid mahself no mo'. Ah means tuh make Sam take me fishin' wid him after this. Nobody [i.e., the negative community of women and the signifying men] better not criticize yuh in mah hearin'" (182–83). Pheoby responds excitedly to Janie's call to break with hierarchies of representations and to stop seeing herself as a silent subject. It is significant to point out that Janie comes to Pheoby religiously speaking, from a point of strength, not coping. She knows who her God is. She does not seek confirmation for her actions, but affirmation of voice. The religious imagination of the community enters into Janie's verbal consciousness and shapes her response to historical pressures.

The language of the black church is a communal language invested with authority. Not only does this communal language give Janie voice and legitimacy, but it also sustains her. Through it, she can prevent the memory of Tea Cake from dying. The connection to romance—a vertical language—becomes apparent to the mesmerized Pheoby as well as to the reader-participant. Janie's ritual retelling of her journey toward the horizon enables her to suspend the rules of time and space as she moves toward the climactic moment in her sermon—the tragic death of her beloved Tea Cake. Each time Janie tells of their short but intense life together, she relives the experience, much as Christians do when they participate in the Eucharist. In fact *Their Eyes Were Watching God* may be viewed as a series of revelations leading toward ultimate revelation—Janie's being reunited in the spirit with Tea Cake.

The novel ends where it began, within the perceptual field of the narrator, who releases it from the temporal world. In this way, Janie and Tea Cake achieve a greater freedom in the world tomorrow, and Janie triumphs over her critics, the negative community of gossiping women to whom the reader is introduced in the book's opening sequence. With her spiritual loyalties no longer divided, Janie, in a picture at least as arresting as the novel's opening scene, draws the various strands of her sermon together: "She pulled in her horizon like a great fish-net. Pulled it from around the waist of the world and draped it over her shoulder. So much of life in its meshes! She called in her soul to come and see" (184). In pulling the fishnet around her shoulder, Janie arrests the "eschatological despair."[19] An optimist and a romantic, Janie seeks a larger space for herself and her life's story; her quest involves woman's timeless search for freedom and wholeness. Her charge to her new convert is "you got tuh *go* there tuh *know* there" (183). Janie, in her movement toward the horizon (i.e., the successful execution of her performance via the sermon), is transformed from blues figure to prophet. In moving toward this transformation, she both achieves personal fulfillment and assumes a communal role traditionally reserved for males. She appropriates tropes of creation ("She had given away everything in their little house except a package of garden seed that Tea Cake had bought to plant" [182]) and reunion ("She pulled in her horizon like a great fish-net") in order to insert her voice into history.[20]

In the end, Janie's sermon becomes a poetry of affirmation—with self, community, and loved ones. Janie and Pheoby are uplifted through the preached word. Operating from a position of strength within the ethos of her community, Janie achieves an unspeakable intimacy that bonds her to her community of faith.

19. Kermode, *Sense of an Ending*, 9.

20. For a critique of the "prophetic moment" as a distinctly male enterprise, see James Krasner, "Zora Neale Hurston and Female Autobiography."

4

The Sermon without Limits and the Limits of the Sermon

Invisible Man

One of the distinguishing features of Ralph Ellison's critically acclaimed *Invisible Man* is his rich use of folk materials as a means of commenting on the complexity of life for modern man. He has been much praised for the richness and vitality of Afro-American speech in his dialogue and for the virtuosity of his integration of blues and jazz motifs. Bernard Bell notes that Ellison "sees the blues singer and jazz musician as paradigms of the American experience. Both are products of the interaction between the limitations and possibilities of the American experience."[1] I would add the preacher to these two figures, making a trinity. Nurtured in the same soil, he stands at the apex of the experience.

The sermon as a rhetorical mode provides a broad enough perspective for Ellison to provide the substance and insights of the experiences of his ostensibly naive protagonist, the unnamed Invisible Man. The protagonist's experiences serve as a metaphor for black people's experiences in general. They are caught in an unending cycle wherein they must constantly live and write history at the same time. They struggle in vain to see, in the words of Paul, "through a glass darkly" (1 Cor. 13:12). But at best, they see no clear image. (This is underscored by Ellison's many references in the

1. Baker, *Blues, Ideology, and Afro-American Literature*, 111–12, and Bell, *Afro-American Novel*, 204.

novel to phantoms, nightmares, and dreams.) Blacks are a cacophony of voices, existing as figments of the imagination of the dominant culture. The ritual dimension of the sermon orders their reality, encodes similarities, and rescues them from the painful gaze of a world that looks on "in amused contempt and pity."[2] In this chapter I will examine Ellison's use of biblical motifs and sermonic rhetoric in *Invisible Man,* with specific reference to the prologue-epilogue, Trueblood, Rev. Barbee's speech at the college, and the unnamed protagonist as preacher. I will address the question of how these passages expand and amplify each other.

Ellison shows us that, however complicated and supressed the tradition of black cultural forms such as blues, spirituals, folk rhymes, and black sermons, they maintain a vital relation to the black sermonic tradition, its voice and vision. The narrative tension in *Invisible Man* grows out of the narrator's desire to move into the mainstream without acknowledging these cultural forms in his history. Paradoxically, he draws on the verbal forms produced by that suppressed tradition to bring himself into focus and to establish an identity of which he can be proud. During his pre-invisible days, the Invisible Man was like that "religious figure the trickster, who has the power to create but no sense of how to create."[3] The Invisible Man's creation is the text.

The once ambitious Invisible Man implies that when he emerges from his underground hole, he will be ready to challenge the rules of the game, the mythos that imprisons him and wraps him in invisibility, which is given expression in the storefront preacher's sermon as the "blackness of blackness."[4] That he strives to liberate himself from other people's definition of reality (history) is what distinguishes the unnamed narrator from his grandfather, Douglass, who, as we shall see, is the touchstone that brings his problematic encounters all together. Douglass learned that the key to success lies in how effectively one can project oneself beyond the rules of the game, society's prescribed rituals, which makes seizing the word a delicious form of imaginative play. What the Invisible Man lost sight of during his pre-invisible days was that his desire

2. Du Bois, *Souls of Black Folk,* 5.

3. Long, *Significations,* 137.

4. Ellison, *Invisible Man,* 9. All further references to this work are noted by page number in parentheses.

for upward mobility is the hidden bond between art and power. Hence, as he spins the emotional moment, he makes frequent references to preacher and bluesman and their ability to be nimble and inventive.

Under a narcotic trance, the unnamed protagonist passes in illusion into his slave past. He sees the dynamics that went into the creation of a shared value system among blacks: the auction block, an old black woman who killed her white master because he did not free her and their two sons, and the storefront preacher, who gives meaning to blackness. This illusory journey back reveals *how* the blues, spirituals, folk rhymes, and black sermons came into existence; his experience, which he gives us in the narrative, provides him with the answer to *why* these aesthetic forms must exist in such a dynamically charged state. In their most fundamental state, these aesthetic forms, which share a common myth of origins, must be about liberation.

The prologue-epilogue encloses the Invisible Man's "testimonial." The reader must accept it as a measure of how far he has grown. In terms of narrative strategy, the framework, as Raymond Hedin notes, relegates his "experiences" to the status of middle, defined, as all literary middles are, by its relationship to the beginning and the end, thus creating the impression that the narrative proper is a "means" serving the sufficiently enlightened narrator's "ends." The prologue-epilogue as frame signals the intentions of the narrator to share his experiences, his discovery of self and of a voice and vision that will give expression to his discovery. It signals his bonding with his aesthetic community and the maturation of his autobiographical voice. He is a witness to the integrity of the folk vision while he signals his intent to build upon it, for in the final analysis he affirms "his own identity as an individual who is black, American, and above all human."[5]

The epilogue is in the tradition of the preacher's exhortation to the wayward sinner to "close off" the sinner's stories of his or her abject past and "open up" a new chapter in his or her life. The Invisible Man holds out a promise of renewed action following years of inaction. Constituting the broad middle of his life, the

5. "Strategies of Form in the American Slave Narrative," 25–35. The following discussion of the prologue-epilogue as "testimonial" proceeds in terms of this essay. See also Ladell Payne, *Black Novelists and the Southern Literary Tradition*, 97.

"text" is "confessional" in that the Invisible Man describes his complicity in his debasement. He uses the epilogue to confirm his higher calling and to close off any suspicion that he had fled simply to serve himself. He embraces social ends in order to put an end, once and for all, to the question of his humanity, which is inseparable from his invisibility. The force of his story is predicated on his claim that his story is not unique, that it represents countless others as well:[6] "Who knows but that, on the lower frequencies, I speak for you?" (568).

The end of the identity quest in Ellison's fiction betrays the beginning—black people's violent history, which causes them to stand outside of official American history. As a result, they are rendered invisible; they, therefore, must search within themselves for the answers they seek in the world of the Other. Ellison depicts this world as one of swirling chaos. Black expressive culture represents the attempt on the part of the community to order the chaos. The quest for manhood is the quest for identity. From the black male perspective, the quest for manhood, freedom, and literacy are ritualized in folk forms because they so accurately express the conflict between black manhood and white power in American society.[7]

The unnamed hero's new definition of self, as is evident in the prologue-epilogue, is linked to the rhetorical skills that win him early recognition, first as a high school orator, then as a political speaker. The social and intellectual values of his college are symbolized by Rev. Barbee's style. The political techniques and the propaganda of the Brotherhood demand special rhetorical methods, while Ras, the Brotherhood's archenemy, establishes a formidable reputation as the emotionalist "Exhorter" of Harlem.[8] These are the fields of possibility open to him as he seeks to break a historical cycle that threatens to return him to one segment of the black historical past, namely, slavery. Hence his frequent references to a "boomerang" of history (6). Nestled safely beneath the city and with a newfound awareness, Ellison's narrator begins the healing process.

In the prologue-epilogue, he speaks no longer as one of limited

6. Hedin, "Strategies of Form," 29–30.

7. Susan L. Blake, "Ritual and Rationalization: Black Folklore in the Works of Ralph Ellison," 122.

8. Lloyd W. Brown, "Ralph Ellison's Exhorters: The Role of Rhetoric in *Invisible Man*," 289.

voice and vision. He speaks with the accent of the preacher and appears as the fallen man in his religious discourse as "a condition of liberating practice." The sermon as liberating social practice enables him to insert his voice into history and to close the gap in the alienating social power that renders him politically impotent (expressed in the narrative as his elusive desire to be a leader). Ironically, for the better part of his life he finds himself alienated from those constituencies in whose name he speaks.[9]

Ellison's nameless narrator is both insider and outsider, yet what stamps him as 'insider' is his command over the "language of religion," the precision and coherence of which being the test of his depth of understanding of the community he has at times heavily criticized. His capacity to signify on the community is also greatly enhanced by his command of the language of religion. If one accepts the language of "religion as a system of social tokens and identifications,"[10] then Ellison's protagonist uses this language in terms of the moral obligations it lays upon him (and by extension the reader). He uses its authority and social power as a badge of identification with which his very existence is called into question. Moreover, he needs this language as his natural and spontaneous mode of *self*-identification.

He needs a language that defines him in terms of social authority. In the prologue-epilogue, he presents himself as conversant with the language of religion as a dominant mode of authority in his community, while in between—in his fall from innocence into experience—he disrupts this language that presents itself, as Denys Turner observes, as the "natural and spontaneous mode of thought." In short, the Invisible Man challenges the ideology of the preacher in a priest-dominated community and points out the "performance contradictions." The variety of preachers whom the Invisible Man encounters provide Ellison with the opportunity to critique black leadership or, more precisely, the black leadership model as defined by the historic black church. Concerns over this leadership style and its appropriateness for leading the New Negro into a new century provide the subtext for the spirited Washington-Du Bois debate.[11]

9. Dirlik, "Culturalism as Hegemonic Ideology," 47–48.

10. Denys Turner, *Marxism and Christianity,* 41, 40.

11. Turner, "Ideology and Contradiction," in *Marxism and Christianity,* 24–37. Among the first to popularize the term *New Negro* was none other than the princi-

The sermonic rhetoric bridges the gap between the priest-governing cultural workers and their disenfranchised community. The preacher's familiar refrain "Everybody is a child of God" masks the class tensions and competing interests in the black community. Stepping inside the language of religion, the Invisible Man presents himself as *naturally* congruent with the desires of the corporate community. This is how he masks the contradiction between *is* and *ought,* between arrogant individualism and communal vision—a vision that takes into account the "blackness of blackness." As he surveys his life, the Invisible Man in his narrative posture positions himself as being in harmony with the voice and vision of his community, defined as heroic struggle and overcoming. The sermon, conservative discourse that it is, is recognizable and understood by members of his aesthetic community. It thus grants him an entrée into that community. Furthermore, the Invisible Man as trickster figure and virtuoso expects us to judge him by his lofty standards.

The Blackness of Blackness

The storefront preacher celebrates the heroic side of black life that is often crushed under the weight of machine culture in the urban metropolis. This captivating figure sketches in broad outlines the human desire to belong and anchors it to the world behind the veil, in which black people feel the weight of their ignorance, "not simply of letters," as Du Bois poignantly divined, "but of life, of business, of the humanities; the accumulated sloth and shirking and awkwardness of decades and centuries shackled hands and feet."[12] At its most basic level, the preacher's sermon, infused with evangelical Christianity, acknowledges the violent beginnings of black people's life in America—that history which the nameless hero wants to repress in his quest for identity. The storefront preacher's sermon is more suggestive than the prescriptive one delivered by Rev. Homer A. Barbee on Founder's Day at a southern black college.

The storefront preacher, who exemplifies the "primitive" expres-

pal of Tuskegee, Booker T. Washington, in *The Future of the American Negro* (1899) and in *A New Negro for a New Century* (1900). For a look at the intellectual history associated with this term, see Wilson Jeremiah Moses, "The Lost World of the Negro, 1895–1919: Black Literary and Intellectual Life before the 'Renaissance.'"

12. Du Bois, *Souls of Black Folk,* 9.

siveness of the black peasant, is the type of preacher the bourgeois-leaning Invisible Man reflects on during Barbee's Founder's Day sermon, which is full "of that wild emotion of the crude preachers most of us knew in our home towns and of whom we were deeply ashamed" (109). That wild emotion of which the unnamed narrator speaks adds to his estrangement from the community that he wants to lead.

Let us consider the mythological pattern and ritual dimension of the creation story on the congregation in the storefront preacher's sermon, the "Blackness of Blackness":

> And a congregation of voices answered: "That blackness is most black, brother, most black . . ."
> "In the beginning . . ."
> "At the very start," they cried.
> " . . . there was blackness . . ."
> "Preach it . . ."
> " . . . and the sun . . ."
> "The sun, Lawd . . ."
> " . . . was bloody red . . ."
> "Red . . ."
> "Now black is . . ." the preacher shouted.
> "Bloody . . ."
> "I said black is . . ."
> "Preach it, brother . . ."
> " . . . an' black ain't . . ."
> "Red, Lawd, red: He said it's red!"
> "Amen, brother . . ."
> "Black will git you . . ."
> "Yes, it will . . ."
> "Yes, it will . . ."
> " . . . an' black won't . . ."
> "Naw, it won't!"
> "It do . . ."
> "It do, Lawd . . ."
> " . . . an' it don't."
> "Halleluiah . . ."
> " . . . It'll put you, glory, glory, Oh my Lawd, in the WHALE'S BELLY."
> "Preach it, dear brother . . ."
> " . . . 'an make you tempt . . ."
> "Good God a-mighty!"
> "Old Aunt Nelly!"

"Black will make you . . ."
"Black . . ."
" . . . or black will un-make you."
"Ain't it the truth, Lawd?" (9–10)

In that it provocatively echoes the opening chapters of Genesis, the storefront preacher's sermon, the "Blackness of Blackness," has epic depth and lyric intensity. Ellison presents the storefront preacher as a representative man, and the sermon he preaches provides an insight into the spirit of the people. He represents the deeper values and emotions of the folk. The preacher and his aesthetic community are unified because the constant reminders of black people's slave past—restricted spatial movement and substandard housing—kept alive in the present do not permit the racial memory to forget how the community has had to compromise itself in order to survive. His mascon-filled sermon affirms and confronts life's fundamental contradictions; it encodes similarities, not differences.

The gestalt of the worship experience enables the aesthetic community to fill in the gaps imaginatively and to make connections that the preacher leaves unconnected. "Indeed, it is only through inevitable omissions that a story will gain its dynamism." The storefront preacher's monosyllabic sermon provokes certain expectations, which in turn the aesthetic community (as well as the reader-spectator) projects onto the text (sermon) in such a way that we reduce the polysemous possibilities to a single interpretation in keeping with the expectations aroused, thus extracting an individual, configurative meaning.[13]

The preacher converts the ordinary living of his downtrodden people to a spiritual advantage; preacher and people sing of their common condition with a common consciousness. This is self-evident in the spirited call-and-response that influences the building of the sermon. The preacher steps inside the community's sense of time and brings to the surface the suppressed cultural values, as he and the people empty language and fill it anew; that is, they impose through language their moral vision of the world.[14] Though black and white preachers *use* the same language, they do not *speak* the same language, for the power that drives the black sermon is the

13. Wolfgang Iser, "The Reading Process: A Phenomenological Approach," 282–83.
14. Barthold, *Black Time.*

people's knowledge that their encounter with God is markedly different than that of the dominant community, expressed in the sermon as "Black will make you . . . or black will un-make you."

The preacher and the people imaginatively "play" with the exemplary pattern of the creation story, with its repetition, its break with profane duration, and its integration into primordial time. The miracle that Ellison celebrates with the storefront preacher and Barbee and that he implies in the epilogue is that the sustaining genius of unlettered and semiliterate black folk preachers is that they did not permit the people to die spiritually. This constitutes the unsaid that the protagonist hears in Louis Armstrong's lyrics and overhears in the storefront preacher's sermon. What unites the storefront preacher, Armstrong, and Ras (to whom the Invisible Man makes a passing reference) is their ability to transform a hermeneutics of domination and suppression into story and song, the making of art. It is a language that reveals the inner depths of the American experience and calls into question the American mode of orientation that conceals black people and renders them invisible.

The incantatory, mantra-like repetition of "In the beginning," as Mircea Eliade informs us, taps into the people's fervent belief that one day there will be a classless society; "the consequent disappearance of all historical tensions find their most exact precedent in the myth of the Golden Age which, according to a number of traditions, lies at the beginning and the end of History." As myth, the creation story is thought to express the absolute truth because it narrates a sacred story, in the holy time of the beginnings. In the retelling of this exemplary story, the black preacher permits the people to detach themselves from profane time and magically reenter sacred time, when, paradoxically, time will be no more.[15]

Central to the staying power of the creation story is the belief in a God who created an orderly world and assigned a preeminent place to man among his creatures. The order in this exemplary world is contrasted with the disorder of the world that blacks daily look out upon. God created the world from chaos to cosmos, from disorder to order, from darkness to light; yet Ellison, in a master stroke of irony, has his unnamed protagonist run from the light

15. *Myths, Dreams, and Mysteries,* 25–26.

into the dark in order to see clearly. Thus Ellison engages and rereads texts that the dominant culture holds to be fundamental to its ethos.

Finally, the preacher transports the people from the material world of pain and suffering to a transcendent world, where pain and suffering will be no more. Traditionally, the imaginary world was used as a clue and a tool for the understanding of the concrete world. Ellison reverses this view as he uses the pain and agony of the concrete world to transport the weary travelers in a strange land to a transcendent imaginary world. The preacher thus fashions and reinforces an optimistic vision of the end of history consistent with the imaginative yearnings of his aesthetic community. As myth and ritual, the opening chapters of Genesis ("In the beginning") are consistent with a people's need for regeneration.

The storefront preacher's sermon becomes the paradigmatic text against which all other texts are measured. The Invisible Man, as participant-narrator, gains his voice (presence) not only by engaging the Other through his mastery of formal English in the construction of his text (the novel) but also by openly signifying on the paradigmatic text of the storefront preacher: the "blackness of blackness."

The Invisible Man signifies on what the storefront preacher does not say, what the blind Homer A. Barbee cannot say, and what the cunning Rinehart dares not say: that this pleasant world of known truths is rooted in exploitation and oppression and domination. The picture of Douglass in the office of the Brotherhood stands as a mute reminder to this truth. Under the guise of an antiestablishment act of smoking marijuana, the ostensibly naive narrator forces the reader-spectator out of his or her customary and comfortable position into painful confrontations with unsuspected truths. Unlike the storefront preacher, whose mandate is to verbalize something that is not of a verbal nature—man's and woman's creatureliness before the Creator—the Invisible Man, no longer suffering from a perverse opacity, presents his unsuspecting reader with a critique of a properly materialistic philosophy that has the same force and doom as that of the oppressive dread of the religious experience. To grasp the point of Ellison's inclusion of the storefront preacher in the prologue is in this sense to grasp his vision of the African in American history.

God of Our Weary Years, God of Our Silent Tears

Ellison uses the edenic vesper scene in chapter 5 to celebrate the peerless artistry of the black preacher and to critique a particular kind of black leadership for its promotion of a narrow vision. In spite of its grandeur, the black sermon, for Ellison (like all aesthetic objects such as paintings, statues, and artifacts), can only come into existence through a process of alienation and estrangement within human society. This thesis is fully developed in the spectacular sermon given by the blind Homer A. Barbee—who in spite of his spellbinding performance directs the energies of his enraptured audience toward conformity. The name for social reality is passed off as democracy, free enterprise, and progress. In retrospect, the unnamed participant-narrator now realizes that Barbee's sermon was as much a part of his socialization as was the Battle Royal ("Be aware of the boomerang of history"). The stirring words of James Weldon Johnson's "Negro National Anthem" provide the subtext for this race ritual, and Du Bois's *Souls of Black Folk* serves as the silent text.[16]

The occasion is Founder's Day at a state college for blacks in a nameless southern state, and Barbee's mission on this occasion is to deliver an emotionally enriching eulogy venerating the name of the institution's Founder and first President. The Founder, modeled on Booker T. Washington (a Moses type), is the illustrious leader who, through education and uplift, would lead his people out from beneath the foot of the white majority. As he executes his mission, the preacher responds to the aspirations of his audience, engages their imagination, and raises their spiritual forces.

Through his verbal art, Barbee combats the terror of the world outside. Preaching, therefore, is an act of riding the terror—much in the same way the blues singer worries the word. As dream keeper and dream maker, Barbee both arrests the despair the outside world encourages and marshals the audience's spiritual forces to withstand it. Through his joyful-mournful rhapsody, Barbee extracts beauty from a harrowing experience. To preach the Lord's word in a strange land means never to permit the people to stop

16. "Lift Every Voice and Sing," 32–33. In his autobiography, Johnson tells of the ecstasy that overcame him during the composition of this song, which is commonly known as the Black National Anthem. See *Along This Way,* 154–55.

dreaming; the result would be a failure of courage and the death of the spirit. To sustain the redemptive dream of the promised land is an integral part of black America's cultural heritage that is handed down from generation to generation by active tradition bearers such as Homer A. Barbee. Like his predecessors, Barbee keeps hope alive with his constant reminders that black people have a God, in the words of James Weldon Johnson, a "God of our weary years" and a "God of our silent tears."

Barbee's electrifying sermon is not only a variation on the storefront preacher's sermon, the "Blackness of Blackness," but it also extends the observation that the Invisible Man recalls Louis Armstrong making about the blueness of blackness in his incisive recording "Black and Blue." Barbee's pietistic Christian sermon in praise of the Founder cannot mute the blues ethos that colors his audience's vision. His challenge is to rechannel the latent anger, frustration, and rejection that simmer in the souls of black folk. He skillfully draws upon his art form to emphasize altruism and conformity over rebellion and revolution.

To put Barbee's sermon into perspective and to evaluate the relationship between the spiritual and the blues vision as alternative perspectives on the solution to the problem of creating meaning from black suffering, it is necessary to revisit the terrible blues of Jim Trueblood, which precede Barbee's sermon as the irreducible bass beat of black life. The blues are the sermon without limits, and the sermon is the blues with limits.

Daily crushed under the weight of an exploitative ideology, Jim Trueblood, a sharecropper, rises above his anonymity through an incestuous relationship with his daughter. The incestuous act symbolizes all that is wrong with a system that is all take and no give. Inexplicably, Trueblood, excluded from polite black society, discovers fame and fortune in his infamous deed. From far and near, the whites, bearing gifts, make a pilgrimage to his one-room shack, encouraging him to tell his story again and again. Driving aimlessly—or perhaps with more aim than he knows—the unnamed hero commits the unpardonable sin of taking a philanthropic white trustee, Mr. Norton, away from the "whitewashed" campus to the backwoods homestead of Trueblood. The hero would like to leave, but Norton, curiously fascinated by the fact that Trueblood has committed incest (and survived), insists on talking with the sharecropper. At Norton's prodding, Trueblood tells his story, an extended and graphically detailed account of how he was induced by a dream into having physical relations with his daughter.[17]

Reduced to performing for his livelihood, Trueblood addresses a white world in a black vernacular. As man and as symbol, he articulates the ritualized pain of a segment of the black community; Barbee articulates that of the other. Trueblood's themes are infinite human potential blocked, racial inequality, exploitation, and bankrupt religious values. As he has done on previous occasions, Trueblood wrestles authorial control from Norton, the latest pilgrim to his shrine, and "silences" the discomforted participant-narrator, who is also struggling to find his voice. Trueblood speaks through an ironic, self-conscious voice, appropriating proverbial wisdom, which is clearly the possession of a tradition rather than an individual, and transforming it into a discourse that is as much an account of poetry as it is an account of the world (read: the terror of history). Trueblood plays upon Norton's emotions as though he were sliding his fingers across a finely tuned guitar. Unable to break the spell Trueblood casts over Norton, the hero can do nothing except marvel at his performance: "Trueblood seemed to smile at me behind his eyes as he looked from me to the white man and continued" (60).

Trueblood's blues arise out of his need to define self and form. Material conditions shape his blues. In this sense, we can say that he is true to the conditions that made him; he does not deny his history. In that Trueblood converts his history into a self-conscious production, he performs a ritual function. His authority rests upon rituals that grew out of the slave experience, which include rituals of toil and despair and regeneration. He shows that when the exigencies of the times have demanded poet-prophets, those who were chosen did not always wear the covering mantle of institutional authority.

Ever the sensitive artist, Trueblood skillfully shows the mesmerized Norton and the embarrassed participant-narrator, who represents

17. Spillers, "'The Permanent Obliquity of an In(pha)llibly Straight': In the Time of the Daughters and the Fathers." Spillers offers a provocative reading of the incest theme in *Invisible Man* and other African American texts. She observes that "fictions about incest provide an enclosure, a sort of confessional space for and between postures of the absolute . . . and in a very real sense it is only in fiction . . . that incest as dramatic enactment and sexual economy can take place at all" (128).

the silent majority in upwardly mobile black America, that man's dignity and identity rest upon a religious commitment. To the question raised by the preacher in the institutional church, is there life after death?, Trueblood, ever the hard-nosed realist, responds with: where is the love in this absurd world? The former looks in the text of Scripture, where the liberating word is to be found, while the latter looks in the text of the blues, where one must confront the pain and terror of history in order to claim his or her freedom. As Trueblood puts it to the youngblood, to make it through this vale of tears, you got to learn "to move without movin'" (59).

In the defiant agony of his misery, Trueblood asserts his right to be, in effect, to challenge the Judeo-Christian view that one's arms are too short to box with God.[18] He snatches victory from certain defeat by wrestling with life on its own terms. His complaint is that he is forced to violate those that he loves in exchange for a grotesque respectability. Trueblood's virtue is his uncompromising defiance. His life is the unvarnished reality that will not be hidden in the inner springs of lofty words; it lends specificity to the "blackness of blackness," and it brings into focus the contradictions in Barbee's sermon.

Ellison's blind Homer A. Barbee stands in a long line of the old-time black folk preachers, those black and unknown bards who—through the power of their words—elevated the spirits and steeled the will of a downtrodden people. A precursor for Ellison's Barbee may be seen in the depiction of Rev. Simpson in Dunbar's *The Uncalled.* He is physically unattractive. When he preaches at the funeral of Fred Brent's mother, he attempts, as Dunbar makes clear, to stir emotion rather than to give insight. Another precursor to Barbee may be seen in Johnson's *Autobiography of an Ex-Coloured Man,* near the end of the novel, where the narrator describes the preacher. Johnson makes one of the few favorable references to the exhorter found in the early novel.[19]

18. Throughout the discussion with his friends on the mystery of suffering, Job continually asks why misfortune has happened to him, a good, upright man. In his first discourse from the Whirlwind, the Lord offers such a man the right to challenge the divine rule. He then stuns Job into silence and submission with a series of rhetorical interrogations, including "Hast thou an arm like God? or canst thou thunder with a voice like him?" (Job 40:9)

19. Palosaari, "Image of the Black Minister." See also Daniel, *Images of the Preacher.*

These exhorters are direct descendants of the classic black folk preacher whom James Weldon Johnson describes in his preface to *God's Trombones.* With the realization that he is quickly losing his audience, and exhausted from a day of marathon meetings in Kansas City, this frustrated preacher discards his prepared text in favor of a more familiar one. Johnson, the bone-tired executive director of the National Association for the Advancement of Colored People, notes the transformation:

> He was at once a changed man, free, at ease and masterful. He was wonderful in the way he employed his conscious and unconscious art. He strode the pulpit up and down in what was actually a very rhythmic dance, and he brought into play the full gamut of his wonderful voice, a voice—what shall I say?—not of an organ or a trumpet, but rather of a trombone, the instrument possessing above all others the power to express the wide and varied range of emotions encompassed by the human voice—and with greater amplitude.[20]

The authenticating voice of the black preacher is given full expression in Barbee's virtuoso performance on Founder's Day. By "authenticating voice," I mean that Barbee's sermon is the centerpiece of a carefully constructed narrative system; that is, it merges past, present, and future as Barbee "employs his conscious and unconscious art" to structure the meaning of the "Blackness of Blackness" (9). It demonstrates the centrality of the influence of the black sermon as a source for organizing black social reality and as an emotionally enriching system of communication. Barbee, like other black preachers historically, is invested with the cultural authority that permits him to serve as a link between a dependent and defensive black community and a powerful and often hostile white community. In other words, the preacher uses the same language to serve these two often contradictory forces. More often than not, his role calls for him to create a vent, to compromise or provide, during tension-filled moments, an alternate route to rebellion or accommodation. In this way, the preacher fulfills the historic role as "leader/prophet, interpreter/hierophant, orator/actor, symbolist/healer."[21] Accordingly, Barbee, an authentic folk figure, strikes a

20. *God's Trombones,* 6–7.
21. Spillers, "Fabrics of History," 10.

responsive chord in his congregation through preaching as *celebration* and *proclamation* as he joyously retells how the Founder "got ovah." In *The Recovery of Preaching,* Henry Mitchell defines *celebration* as

> both the literal and the symbolic or ritual expression of praise or joy. It may be in regard to an event or a person, historical or legendary, past or present; or it may relate to an object or a belief. A part of the genius of black preaching has been its capacity to generate this very kind of celebration, despite the hardest of circumstances. This genius for celebration is partly responsible for the fact that enslaved and otherwise oppressed blacks have survived the seemingly unbearable.[22]

To the uninitiated, the word *celebration* is associated with the stereotypical rhetorical and stylistic features associated with the black preacher. The often-heard criticism is that the *proclamation,* or the preacher's message, suffers in comparison to the apparently ostentatious "performance." In Barbee, Ellison combines the best of celebration (style) and proclamation (content).

Gerald Lewis Davis recognizes celebration as the mainspring of African American performance: "During a performance . . . both 'performer' and 'audience' are actively locked in a dynamic exchange. . . . Indeed, the demands of the African-American audience for virtuosity and dynamic invention in the performance of a recognized form precludes the performer's adherence to the static reproduction of familiar and popular narrative forms."[23]

In other words, even as Barbee engages and manipulates the highly charged symbolic language of the black sermon, his aesthetic community demands that his performance be "dynamic and inventive." However, Davis continues, "the responsibility for engaging and manipulating the several components of the African-American performance environment is not the performer's alone." The audience participation "drives" the performer to seek "the most effective, consistent and innovative 'reading' of a narrative event" (e.g., the heroic accomplishments of the Founder in a rigidly segregated South).[24]

Barbee creates the climate for celebration through "his voice round

22. *The Recovery of Preaching,* 5.
23. *I Got the World in Me,* 26.
24. Ibid., 27.

and vibrant" (118) and his gestures, his reading of the history of black people "as a 'Jeremiad'—the song of a Fallen man,"[25] and with his constant reminders to the audience of their familiarity with the details of the Founder's life. These strategies serve to collapse the distinction between performer and audience. Once the dormant cultural values are released, the proclamation takes place. The sermon creates a vent in an untenable situation; it mobilizes people to achieve a common social goal. Through his ritual action, Barbee creates a value free of the structures of domination (which, of course, is undercut when he trips over the feet of Dr. Bledsoe); consequently, he enables parents and students to free themselves symbolically from what they must passively endure in the day-to-day.

Before Barbee utters a single word, the youthful narrator paints an unpleasant picture of him. He describes him along the lines of racial stereotypes, almost a caricature of the old-time black folk preacher: Barbee "is a man of striking ugliness, fat, with a bullet-head set on a short neck, with a nose much too wide for its face, upon which he wore black-lensed glasses" (115). He makes Barbee physically unattractive to undercut his integrity (as if one were dependent on the other) before Barbee even speaks. The upwardly mobile narrator informs us that Barbee is the atypical speaker for this momentous occasion:

> I remember the evenings spent before the sweeping platform in awe and in pleasure, and in the pleasure of awe; remember the short formal sermons intoned from the pulpit there, rendered in smooth articulate tones, with calm assurance purged of that wild emotion of the crude preachers most of us knew in our home towns and of whom we were deeply ashamed, these logical appeals which reached us more like the thrust of a firm and formal design requiring nothing more than the lucidity of uncluttered periods, the lulling movement of multisyllabic words to thrill and console us. (109)

Though Barbee does not give a "short formal sermon" like that of his learned counterparts, this is not to say that his sermon lacks form. Also, it is definitely not sterile, guaranteed to put one to sleep (or to let one think about a secret rendezvous among the honeysuckle).

25. Spillers, "Fabrics of History," 2.

Ellison describes how the sermon begins: This "black little Buddha began speaking, his voice round and vibrant as he told of his pleasure in being allowed to visit the school once more after more than many years" (116). Barbee's codified series of gestures and physical movements engage "a slow, rhythmic rocking; tilting forward on his toes until it seemed he would fall, then back on his heels" (116). His physical rhythm corresponds to his verbal rhythm: "And as he tilted he talked until a rhythm was established." This rhythm signals that this authentic folk figure is striking a responsive mythology through black preaching as celebration and proclamation. Thus, he prepares his audience of young persons and gray-headed trustees to make the journey with the role-model Founder, step by painful step.

The surging rhythms of Barbee's sermon transport the audience back to the Founder's heroic struggle of yesteryear, and the preacher merges past, present, and future as he graphically re-creates the life of this exemplary figure who once stood before "this barren land after emancipation . . . this land of darkness and sorrow, of ignorance and degradation, where the hand of brother had been turned against brother, father against son, and son against father; where master had turned against slave and slave against master; where all was strife and darkness, an aching land" (116).

Barbee's introduction establishes the mood and creates rhythm—the rhythm of the King James Bible. Barbee's flair for the dramatic echoes and reechoes the drama of the opening chapters of Genesis. Prior to the Founder's arrival, the South is the "land of darkness and sorrow . . . where all was strife and darkness." This former chaos is implicitly counterbalanced with the present edenic setting of the college—"scents of lilac, honeysuckle and verbena, and the feel of spring greenness" (107). That the sermon is part of a rich oral tradition is indicated by the rhetorical use of balance, repetition, and parallelism ("father against son, and son against father"). The short staccato sentences that are separated by commas and conjunctions serve as registers of the preacher pausing to catch his breath between phrases. They imbue the sermon with a life of its own. Mike Thelwell cogently observes that men of words such as Barbee, who are grounded in a vibrant oral tradition, are past masters of "para-language." He defines it as "gesture, physical expression, and modulation of cadences and intonation which serve to change the meaning—in incredibly subtle ways—of the same collection of words." Like other religious figures, Barbee prepares the people to join him as they create *an*-other reality during their dynamic exchange.[26]

In addition, the narrator reminds us that Barbee's sermon is dominated by monosyllabic words—drawn from the concrete and everyday—as opposed to the multisyllabic words of the typical chapel speaker. The monosyllables create rhythm, and the rhythm gives Barbee power to call forth dormant cultural values, enabling him to make the historical call for freedom, justice, and equality. As his sermon unfolds, it orders the chaos and structures the meaning of *blackness*.

Barbee next takes advantage of the people's familiarity with the details of the Founder's life. He graphically recounts the salient features of the Founder's life from cradle to grave. The Founder's biography is the people's biography writ large:

> And into this land came a humble prophet, lowly like the humble carpenter of Nazareth, a slave and a son of slaves, knowing only his mother. A slave born, but marked from the beginning by a high intelligence and princely personality; born in the lowest part of this barren, war-scarred land, yet somehow shedding light upon it where'er he passed through. I'm sure you have heard of his precarious infancy, his precious life almost destroyed by an insane cousin who splashed the babe with lye and shriveled his seed and how, a mere babe, he lay nine days in a deathlike coma and then suddenly and miraculously recovered. You might say that it was as though he had risen from the dead or been reborn. (116–17)

The Founder's humble beginnings are thus associated with the birth of Jesus, an association with light and goodness in the dark and violent Southland. Whereas Jesus calms the stormy waters, the divinely inspired Founder calms the fratricidal discord of a South which, in the midnight of its despair, turns monster and devours its young, black and white. Against all odds, his task is to bind the

26. "Back with the Wind: Mr. Styron and the Reverend Turner," 80. Although what the linguists call "para-language" may lack complicated syntactical structure and vast vocabulary, Thelwell observes that it is very rich in meanings. For notable studies that address how oppressed people use religion to create *an*-other reality, see Weston Le Barre, *The Ghost Dance: Origins of Religion*, Vittorio Lanternari, *The Religions of the Oppressed*, and Long, *Significations*, 158–72.

wounds of father and son and master and slave, and to soothe the emerging class tensions in the black community.

Barbee concludes his introduction by reminding his audience members that the Founder, like Moses, led their parents and grandparents from the dark days of slavery to the joy that comes in the morning. This is indeed the good news: "like that great pilot of ancient times who led his people safe and unharmed across the bottom of the blood-red sea. And your parents followed this remarkable man across the black sea of prejudice, safely out of the land of ignorance, through the storms of fear and anger, shouting, LET MY PEOPLE GO!" (118)

"Let my people go" is the most responsive mascon in the peculiar eschatology of the black church. The promise of the black sermon is that God is at work in all history. The Israelites' victory is transformed into black victory; the preacher's vision becomes the community's vision; and the vicissitudes of the everyday are transcended. The emotionally charged "Let my people go" touches blacks at the very core of the black experience. "Let my people go" evokes other culturally and religiously significant expressions (e.g., "Swing Low, Sweet Chariot") that sweep like fire over the imagination. The impact of Barbee's skillful use of mascon imagery on the psyche of an oppressed people is easily understood, for the rhythm and tempo of the sermon building increases in each joy-filled audience member who communicates his or her fervor to someone else.[27] The parents march to freedom; Barbee and his audience march to build a sermon that will transport them beyond the boundaries of the everyday. As the people go forth in communal celebration, their collective soul looks back and wonders how they got over. Witness the reaction of the skeptical narrator to Barbee's spellbinding performance: "I listened, my back pressing against the hard bench, with a numbness, my emotions woven into his words as upon a loom" (118). The Invisible Man is transported from his pedestrian criticism of Barbee's physical appearance to his concern for the greater good. Barbee's essential message is that altruism is a virtue; infidelity to the Founder's dream is a loss of courage.

The body of Barbee's sermon shares an affinity with the slave narrative. The Founder's life is presented as a series of close calls

27. Hurston, *Sanctified Church*, 91.

and narrow escapes.[28] Barbee recasts the close calls and narrow escapes that characterize the Founder's early years to stroke the egos of the young black students striving to prove their humanity, and of the white trustees, as well, by acknowledging that there were some humane whites during this dark night of the South's soul.

He credits the Founder's narrow escape from a rabid mob to the trickster, a figure congruent with the ethos of his aesthetic community. The supposedly demented old man and woman kept the "humble prophet" alive by turning the world upside down, an idea that foreshadows the Invisible Man's self-revelatory discovery of Rinehart's disguises. Holding his enraptured audience in the palm of his hands, Barbee creates a climate wherein they not only suffer with the Founder but also comfort him during his escape. Rhetorically, the constant reference to the collective "you" adds rhythm and permits them to share in the experience. Later, Barbee will shift to the even more personal "our." Barbee's dramatic compression serves as a reminder that they have all heard the story of the Founder's heroic struggle many times; therefore, Barbee makes their participation in this re-creation all the more real, their purpose all the more significant:

> And you hurried with him full of doubt to the cabin designated by the stranger, where he met that seemingly demented black man . . . You remember that old one, laughed at by the children in the town's square, old, comic-faced, crafty, *cotton*-headed. And yet it was he who bound up your wounds with the wounds of the Founder. He, the old slave, showing a surprising knowledge of such matters—*germology* and *scabology*—ha! ha!—he called it, and what a youthful skill of the hands! (119–20)

Barbee wraps the Founder in the swaddling clothes of the slave community as he places the Founder squarely within the loving arms of its ethos.

Barbee lapses into the vernacular with "*cotton*-headed," "*germology*," and "*scabology*," as he demonstrates the versatility of his voice, God's trombone. This noble rider of words worries the words. He both lives up to the expectations of his aesthetic community and

28. I have in mind classics of the genre, such as Frederick Douglass's *Narrative*, Henry Bibb's *Narrative*, and Harriet Jacobs's *Incidents in the Life of a Slave Girl*.

binds them to his vision. Other examples of binding are the "you remember" and, used elsewhere in the text, "you plunged" and the royal reference to "our skull" and "cleansed our wound." The "ha! ha!" pauses, where Barbee catches his breath, embody Hughes's observation that the black experience is full of "ironic laughter mixed with tears"—the spiritual twin to the sensibility that makes the narrator recall Louis Armstrong's "Black and Blue."[29]

Another example of the trickster figure is the woman who hid the Founder in her chimney:

> "You hid all the following day in the cabin where thirteen slept in three small rooms, standing until darkness in the fireplace chimney, back in all the soot and ashes—ha! ha!—guarded by the granny who dozed at the hearth seemingly without a fire. You stood in the blackness and when they came with their baying hounds they thought her demented. But she knew, she knew! She knew the fire! She knew the fire! She knew the fire that burned without consuming! My God, yes!"
>
> "My God, yes!" a woman's voice responded, adding to the structure of his vision within me. (120)

The woman's response affirms that Barbee's vision is congruent with her reality. The highly charged symbolic language of the sermon enables Barbee to renew the community's call for salvation, redemption, freedom, justice, and equality. Once Barbee awakens these dormant cultural values in the people, his vision replaces the vision of the community. Barbee completes the communion with preacher, people, and God; he translates the present into an acknowledgment of his oneness with the people and the experience. To be sure, like Barlo in *Cane,* Barbee, too, is engaged in the search for voice. However, unlike Barlo, whose dispossessed African remains full of anger and loathing, Barbee mutes the revolutionary aspects of the incidents surrounding the Founder's life.

As previously mentioned, Barbee also strokes the egos of the white trustees. Whites, too, had a part to play in the dramatic escape of the illustrious Founder: "And you went into this town with him and were hidden by the friendly aristocrat one night, and on the next by the white blacksmith who held no hatred—surprising contradictions of the underground. Escaping, yes! Helped by those

29. Langston Hughes, "The Negro Artist and the Racial Mountain," 307. See also Hurston, *Sanctified Church,* 79.

who knew you and those who didn't know. Because for some it was enough to see him; others helped without even that, black and white" (120–21). The emphasis is on cooperation and brotherhood—the preacher as symbolist/healer.

As Barbee nears the climactic moment in his sermon, the once critical Invisible Man goes from skeptic to convert. He respects the preacher's art, his ability to tap into the aesthetic ideology of the community, which insures his prominence as its principal spokesman: "The fat man was playing upon the whole audience without the least show of exertion. He seemed completely composed, hidden behind his black-lensed glasses, only his mobile features gesturing his vocal drama" (121).

Stylistically, Barbee signals that he approaches the point of greatest emotional intensity in his sermon when he leans on the lectern and turns to Dr. Bledsoe. This flair for the dramatic heightens the audience's expectations as he pretends to hold a private conversation with Bledsoe while addressing the entire audience. This section is designed to elicit the greatest dynamic exchange, as Barbee realizes the aesthetic ideal:[30] "You've heard the bright beginning of the beautiful story, my friends. But there is the mournful ending, and perhaps in many ways the richer side. The setting of this glorious son of the morning" (121).

As Barbee enters the eulogy proper, his audience expects him to do more than merely recount the by now familiar details of the last days of the Founder. The audience expects to re-experience the Founder's triumph over the foes of oppression. The ordering process is embedded in the community's ethos, which the life of the Founder exemplifies. Barbee creatively activates familiar motifs—the promised land, the quest for freedom and literacy, the trickster figure, and the Christian victory over evil in a sin-filled world—to invest the lives of the people with meaning and purpose. Barbee knows the ordering and distribution of these elements in his sermon will exercise a tremendous influence on the nature of the dynamic exchanges between preacher and audience. As orator/actor, he also intuitively knows that what you preach (proclamation) is determined by how you preach (celebration).

The style is inseparable from the content. By this I mean that

30. Davis, *I Got the World in Me,* 26–27.

Barbee taps into a responsive mythology to bring forth the "full" concretization of a particular space, slavery. Barbee builds frame by frame upon the reality of slavery expressed in a language that inspires renewal and redemption. In effect, Barbee's sermon "orders" reality for a community whose members' "shattered lives are burdened by impulses the community cannot master or control."[31] He creates meaning from the images of oppression, despair, deprivation, and isolation that populate black sacred and secular expressions.

Celebration is most apparent in Barbee's electrifying reenactment of the changing of the guard from the humble Founder to the arrogant Bledsoe. To summarize, the Founder, a workaholic spreading his dream of uplift far and wide, collapses from exhaustion in a jam-packed auditorium, recovers momentarily to comfort the distressed audience, and dies later on the train. Barbee reminds his attentive audience that Dr. Bledsoe, the trusty lieutenant, had restored order by "stomping out the time with mighty strokes upon the hollow platform, commanding not in words but in the great gut-tones of his magnificent basso" (123). Barbee deftly calls the audience's attention to the requisite of the successful preacher—a magnificent voice, a trained instrument.

Voices resonate within voices as Barbee freezes the moment in his vivid re-creation of how Bledsoe used his voice to still the emotional waters of the panic-stricken audience. Bledsoe led them in song:

> —and they stand, they calm, and with him they sing out against the tottering of their giant. Sing out their long black songs of blood and bones:
>
> "Meaning HOPE!
> "Of hardship and pain:
> "Meaning FAITH!
> "Of humbleness and absurdity:
> "Meaning ENDURANCE!
> "Of ceaseless struggle in darkness, meaning:
> "TRIUMPH . . .
> "Ha!" Barbee cried, slapping his hands, "Ha!
>
> Singing verse after verse, until the leader revived!" (Slap, slap of his hands.)

31. Menakhem Perry, "Literary Dynamics: How the Order of a Text Creates Its Meaning." See also Wright, "Literature of the Negro," 86.

> "Addressed them"—
> (Slap!) "My God, my God!"
> "Assured them"—(Slap!)
> "That"—(Slap!)
> "He was only tired of his ceaseless efforts." (Slap!) "Yes, and dismisses them, sending each on his way rejoicing, giving each a parting handshake of fellowship . . ."
> I watched Barbee pace in a semi-circle, his lips compressed, his face working with emotion, his palms meeting but making no sound. (123–24)

The stylistics of the black preacher are now on display as Barbee powerfully intones his "Train Sermon." The "Train Sermon" refers to a body of sermons "in which," as James Weldon Johnson observes, "God and the devil were pictured as running trains, one loaded with saints, that pulled up in heaven, and the other with sinners, that dumped its load in hell."[32] This sermon allows the preacher the greatest latitude in showing off his stuff, including pacing and timing. Ellison draws upon this sermon in his description of the Founder's death, which climaxes Barbee's eulogy (125–26). Preached again and again, the Train Sermon, like many of the classic black sermons, eventually took on the qualities of a frozen, as opposed to a dynamic, oral text. Even as Ellison celebrated the artistry of the black folk preacher, one cannot help but wonder whether he thought these classic sermons had become objects for aesthetic contemplation—separated from their social mission. Have they become well-wrought urns to be admired and marveled at?

Barbee draws upon the polyphonic nuances of his art: he walks and struts; he moans and groans; and he speaks in staccato sentences, steeped in driving rhythm and rich imagery. He is a peacock with words. In *Black Preaching,* Henry Mitchell points out that critics of black preaching, with some justification, pejoratively refer to the "moaning," "tuning," "zooning," raspy breathing, strutting, and other highly animated gestures as "whoopology."[33] It is fitting that, as Barbee vividly recounts the familiar details of the Founder's last days for his spellbound audience, the youthful narrator calls the

32. Bernard W. Bell, *The Folk Roots of Afro-American Poetry,* 56–57. Bell extends the observations made by Johnson on this classic black sermon. See Johnson, *God's Trombones,* 1–5.

33. *Black Preaching,* 63.

reader's attention to his voice, a trained instrument. It rings out (123), is a clap of thunder (123), sighs off in nostalgia (124), disembodies (124), whispers (125), accelerates (125), rasps (125), and makes a loud silence in the minds of the audience when he pauses momentarily. All of this is by design to make the audience "see the vision" (131).

The "full" concretization of the text/sermon is realized when the mascons explode in the imagination. Barbee skillfully plays upon the mascons in this emotionally charged scene, first to bind his youthful audience to the Founder's dream, and second to heap praise upon Bledsoe, the Founder's hand-picked successor. As the mascons explode in the imagination, the performer and the audience are one. They see, hear, and touch the Founder. Repetition is re-creation. Now the proclamation takes place. The sermon serves as cathartic release from the tyranny of the everyday, as agent for social change—to mobilize the community to reach some common social goal (the Founder's dream). That the exhausted Founder recovers momentarily to give the distressed people some parting words of comfort Barbee uses figuratively to remind them that he (and by implication, Bledsoe) embodied all they hope to be. Barbee thus converts a potentially tragic story into a jubilee song—triumphant, not somber. This communal celebration is the sermonic equivalent to the sensibility joyfully expressed in the rousing spiritual "My Lord, What a Morning."[34]

In his proclamation, Barbee emphasizes altruism and conformity, as opposed to anger and complacency. He mutes those rebellious voices who would strike out at their oppressors. Implicit in his proclamation—he challenges the students and trustees to ask not what the Founder can do for them, but what they can do to see that the Founder's dream shall not perish. He points out that the Founder brought light to the "darkness" of the midnight South and that this darkness will return if they abdicate their socially responsible roles and permit the Founder's dream to be extinguished.

The no longer naive participant-narrator discovers that to be stylistically and rhetorically significant he must, by custom and tradition, be linguistically ambiguous, multivalent—open to a series of interpretations. His earlier ignorance of linguistic ambiguity almost

34. Johnson and Johnson, 1:162–63.

led to his losing the scholarship at the Battle Royal, as he stepped out of character and did not play the socially responsible role. "As a social ritual, the Battle Royal," Susan Blake notes, "reflects the limitation of blackness in the face of white power. As an initiation ritual, it reflects the limitation of youth in the face of maturity."[35]

The Invisible Man's respect for the magic of words is evident as he sits in the Brotherhood's office under the picture of Frederick Douglass and wonders:

> Sometimes I sat watching the watery play of light upon Douglass' portrait, thinking how magical it was that he had talked his way from slavery to a government ministry, and so swiftly. . . . What had his true name been? Whatever it was, it was as *Douglass* that he became himself, defined himself. And not as a boat-wright as he'd expected, but as an orator. Perhaps the sense of magic lay in the unexpected transformations. (372)

The magical transformation of name and character has a biblical precedent. According to his grandfather, "You start as Saul, and end up as Paul" (372).

The Invisible Man no longer accepts himself as a shadowy representation. He must assume responsibility for his life because he is implicated in his inferior status. If growth is the end product of life, then his decision to come out of his hole signals that he intends not only to engage life but also to grow spiritually as a result of insights gained from his self-imposed isolation. Unlike Plato's cave dweller, he will dispense with shadowy representations when he boldly steps forth into the bright light of freedom from his self-imposed hibernation. He will emerge with his newly found awareness that, in spite of systematic denial of his humanity, the most important thing in the world is himself. Whether or not the oppressors will see him becomes a moot point; he will see himself and see how beautiful he is.

Metaphorically, Ellison shows that the process of unification within the black community begins really with self and moves onward with sympathy, identification, and love. The genesis of the Invisible Man as a healing force ties in with the religious symbol to which he makes reference in the epilogue: the Easter chick (resurrection and redemption). He serves notice that he will return anew and signals that, through the purification process, he closes the existential void.

35. "Ritual and Rationalization," 122.

From his hole, the Invisible Man looks deep into the experiences of people such as his grandfather, Trueblood, Mary Rambo, the old couple in Harlem, Brother Tarp, Ras, and Rinehart, as well as his own experience of what it means to be black in America. He discovers and accepts that he is the sum total of these experiences. He concludes that the personal is the public and conjoins his voice to the cultural biography of his community. The humanizing influence of black music that infuses his spiritual odyssey expresses the vitality and diversity of the collective experience of Africans in America. The music serves as a counterweight to a pietistic Christianity, with its moral absolutes.[36]

Like the preacher, the no longer naive narrator now spins the emotional moment as he transforms the discrete aspects of his experience from an embarrassing series of failures to an oral expressive unifying document that conveys a shared value system. For the narrator, the sermon becomes a very sturdy cultural bridge on which he crosses over. In so doing, he demonstrates his reverence for the magic of words.

The importance of the narrator's pose should not be underestimated. Like the preacher, the ostensibly unassuming narrator in effect sucks the unsuspecting reader into his spellbinding story. Denied other avenues in which to express his talents, the narrator turns inward and makes the sermon his own creation. It is the vehicle that orders his experiences and reestablishes his bond with the community. Though he cannot free himself from man-made states of oppression, the Invisible Man's freedom comes in that he is able to imaginatively articulate his experiences.

The problem Ellison articulates here is a perplexing one because, in large measure, he places the responsibility for his unnamed protagonist achieving freedom from oppression on the character's own shoulders, in challenging him to assert his human rights and his free will. The Invisible Man, as a representative voice for his oppressed community, needs a language both to articulate his invisi-

36. Cornel West, *Prophecy Deliverance!: An Afro-American Revolutionary Christianity,* 86. Others who have commented on the humanizing influence of black music include diverse scholars such as: Du Bois, *Souls of Black Folk;* Lovell, *Black Song: The Forge and the Flame;* Harold Courlander, *Negro Folk Music U.S.A.;* Eileen Southern, *The Music of Black Americans;* Cone, *The Spirituals and the Blues;* and Wyatt Tee Walker, *"Somebody's Calling My Name": Black Sacred Music and Social Change.*

bility and to make himself visible, for, as he adamantly reminds us in the epilogue: "I'm invisible, not blind" (563). The sermon equips him with such a language; its telos points toward a utopia whose vision is not socially valid for him. His many references to religious symbols suggest that freedom lies in his ability "to share with society a conception of a future world of possibilities which is concrete and communicable" and which will enable him to transform reality.[37] To be sure, his freedom is linked to the freedom of the black community; nevertheless, he will not permit himself to become enslaved to ideologies that will "close" him off from dialectical thought, as is evident when he throws "the spear that locked [Ras's] jaws" (547) during the riot in Harlem.

While the unsuspecting reader may feel sorry for the ostensibly naive narrator, he, meanwhile, turns the tables as he demonstrates his mastery of the basic rules that give the specific speech act (the sermon) its meaning. Through his act of creation, the Invisible Man rises from personal demoralization to personal triumph; he implicitly claims victory for the corporate community as well as for himself. Furthermore, his linguistic dexterity hints at the artist latent in his personality and what might have been had he not had to labor behind the veil of racism. And finally, the sermon as a creative act enables him to bond himself to the community from which he once ran. His fluency in this oral expressive communal art form enables him to join his vision with the vision of the community.

Extending the observations of Northrop Frye in "Varieties of Literary Utopia," Chester J. Fontenot in "Visionaries, Mystics, and Revolutionaries: Narrative Postures in Black Fiction" asserts, "Only when we are able to distinguish among the three types of utopian thinkers—the visionary, the mystic, and the revolutionary—will we be in a position to unravel the puzzle presented by black writers who adopt a narrative posture which intentionally misleads the reader into considering their writings to be something other than what the nature of those writings reveals."[38] All indications are that the Invisible Man will lean toward the posture of visionary if and when he emerges from his underground (w)hole.

Although Ellison's protagonist does not claim an unmediated

37. Fontenot, "Visionaries, Mystics, and Revolutionaries," 64–69.
38. Ibid., 64. See also Northrop Frye, "Varieties of Literary Utopias," 323.

apprehension of truth (the mystic), he does claim a vision grounded within social tradition that is concrete and communicable to black America. He reworks a communicable but incomplete vision (blacks' desire to be full participants in American society), in an attempt to create a new social and poetic tradition. His comments in the epilogue suggest that he will put forth a vision that will enable him to transform present reality. It will be free of the tyranny of religious fundamentalism and of the self-defeating revolutionary ideal.

In terms of character development, the parade of preachers the naive narrator encounters in his journey from innocence to experience may be viewed as one preacher, one people, black people, dissected. To be sure, it may be argued that preaching as metaphor for black life in America advocates resistance to codes of subordination and domination; nevertheless, the culturally embedded vision which celebrates heroic struggle and overcoming is not always used to advance the welfare of the corporate community.

Thus Ellison sets beside the abject poverty of a Trueblood the beauty and majesty of a Homer A. Barbee. Beside those who rob the sermon of its social context to achieve different social goals (Ras and the Brotherhood), Ellison sets those who possess the sermonic rhetoric yet stand outside its belief system (Rinehart). From the comfort of his hole, the enlightened narrator realizes he just as easily could have become like any one of them. Structurally, the variety of preachers that the nameless narrator encounters attests to the vitality and dynamic character of the sermon in the black community.

In building upon the black aesthetic tradition, Ellison acknowledges his debt to the critical genius of those unknown black bards who recognized that while they were shaped by the material, historical conditions of their existence, their culture also dialectically helped, in its own fashion, to resist that history. The black aesthetic tradition assuaged pain, but it also transgressed, contested, and resisted the overwhelming forces exerted against it. Even though *Invisible Man* is not written in black vernacular, it resonates with the sustaining weight of this culturally rich linguistic tradition.

5

The Sermon as Cultural History

Go Tell It on the Mountain

On Jordan's stormy banks I stand,
And cast a wishful eye
To Canaan's fair and happy land,
Where my possessions lie.
I am bound for the promised land . . .
A Treasury of American Songs

In a now well-documented story, blacks fled an oppressive South by the tens of thousands during the 1920s in search of the promised land. So strong was their desire to escape their penurious existence that they often left behind family and close friends. One remnant of their southern lives that they transplanted North with them was their church. Not only did it serve to keep alive the down-home religion, but the church also stood as buffer between these new arrivals and a cold, antagonistic world as the reality began to dawn upon them that they had merely exchanged one hell for another. Moreover, many who did not feel at home in the mainstream black protestant denominations felt that only their southern churches could provide the right atmosphere for their continued religious growth.

In her study of the work of the black messiah Father Divine in 1930s New York, Sara Harris suggests that the real tragedy of the frustrations that dominated the lives of many blacks who migrated North "lay not in what they did not have but rather in what they could not expect. It was not the reality of their lives that was so unbearable. It was the hopelessness behind the reality." Consequently, many retreated into the sanctuary of the storefront churches to offset their social isolation as they sought liberation from what Olin Moyd describes as "human-caused states and circumstances of oppression as well as salvation from sin and guilt." To be sure, their moods swung back and forth between resignation and hope for redemption. Behind the veil of this religious fundamentalism, they joyously released the "fire that was shut up in their bones."[1]

James Baldwin, in his autobiographical novel *Go Tell It on the Mountain*,[2] lifts the veil on the world of the black storefront church and presents the spiritual energy that binds the black community together as well as the contradictions that it attempts to resolve. *Go Tell* is built out of distinctly African American sensibilities rooted in the black folk church and its peculiar eschatology. Redemption is the root and core motif in this eschatology. In a manner of speaking, *Go Tell* witnesses how the form of the black sermon issued forth directly out of the content of black life. Baldwin's supreme achievement is his use of sermonic language to evoke certain motifs and archetypes familiar to most black Americans. His extensive use of biblical allusions and Christian ritual for symbolic expression have black religion as a point of spiritual departure to tell the tragic story of the black man's lot in America.

The ways in which Baldwin uses black religion as a point of spiritual departure include his incorporation into the very structure of the narrative many sermonic elements associated with the idiom of the black church: the rich oral tradition, the antiphonal call and response, biblical influences and references, vivid imagery, and beautiful metaphors and synonyms; his placement of black music and "expressive spirituality" at the very center of the narrative; and his depiction of the intensity of a religious experience that, as C. Eric Lincoln reminds us, is colored by "the terror and frustration of day-to-day existence in a society in which the oppressor is identified as Christian."[3]

The domestic violence in Baldwin's Grimes family is in large part

1. *Father Divine*, 20, and Moyd, *Redemption in Black Theology*, 7. See also Fauset, *Black Gods of the Metropolis*.

2. All citations refer to the 1953 edition of *Go Tell It on the Mountain* and are noted by page numbers in parentheses.

3. Houston A. Baker, Jr., *Workings of the Spirit: The Poetics of Afro-American Women's Writing*. I borrow the term *expressive spirituality* from Baker's recent study and use it as a means of defusing the pejorative term *emotionalism*. C. Eric Lincoln, *Race, Religion, and the Continuing American Dilemma*, 122.

the result of external pressures brought to bear upon the Grimes family as a result of separate and unequal treatment in the promised land. To be sure, as Shirley S. Allen points out, much of *Go Tell*'s hold on the reader's imagination is "the more universal problem of a youth achieving maturity." Baldwin, therefore, as Carolyn Wedin Sylvander observes, makes it "painfully, dramatically, and structurally clear throughout *Go Tell* that the struggles every individual faces—with sexuality, with guilt, with pain, with love—are passed on, generation to generation."[4]

The point of view in *Go Tell* is skillfully controlled and manipulated to convey the impact of history—personal and collective—on an individual, whether or not that individual is aware of the history. Through a series of flashbacks that serve as reminders that the past is kept alive in the present, Baldwin tells the story of John Grimes's fourteenth birthday. He lives in a Harlem tenement with his parents, younger brother Roy, and two younger sisters, Sarah and Ruth. Through dramatic irony, the characters convict themselves with their very words as they reveal the discrepancy between what they think and how they act. Baldwin sees in the tragic history of black people the role and influence of the public on the private, and, ultimately, as George E. Kent observes, "Baldwin effected a novel that transcended racial and religious categories—became an evoked image of man facing the mysterious universal forces."[5]

And like the preacher, Baldwin enters the symbolic language of the black sermon to produce the "grammar of emotion" as he tells the story of the prostrate sinners who kneel before the altar at the Saturday Tarry Service and pour out their hearts to God. Hortense J. Spillers sees a similarity between this "grammar of emotion (read: exuberance)" and "a tradition of feeling closely akin to rhetorical style." Her observation bears quoting at length:

> In the classical outline, the rhetorical and poetic modes have radically different procedures and ends, i.e., the latter appealing to the emotions, the former to the intellect. These are easy distinctions which doom the two modes of "behavior" to a separate life, but in the black sermon, with its rhetorical flourishes and appeal, with

4. Allen, "Religious Symbolism and Psychic Reality in Baldwin's *Go Tell It on the Mountain*," 173, and Sylvander, *James Baldwin*, 37.

5. "Baldwin and the Problem of Being," 28.

> its various repetitive structures, the two notions are fused. What we have as a result is an "argument" in the garb of rhythm (the sermon chant), various repetitive devices (prosody in the sermon), and numerous figurative/dramatic strategies (use of mimicry and personification; the appropriation of symbols as a way of explaining the world). Since the "argument" demands "enthusiasm," in short, commitment to the idea, the black sermon also defines an attitude which would persuade; together these strategies of development and the disposition which complements them comprise what may be called a "grammar of emotion."[6]

In essence, Baldwin in *Go Tell* utilizes the idiom and the grammar of the black church, which are based on "polyphonic or contrapuntal, rhythmic effects"—the essential element of black sacred and secular music—to increase the *pitch* of his sermon while at the same time maintaining his *variation* on the same theme.[7]

"The Prayers of the Saints," the moral center of the narrative, focuses on a people's need for redemptive love and approval. This preoccupation with the need for approval is a source of considerable anxiety for a bastard people, a people not thought to be made in the image of God, a prostrate community of victims crying out for forgiveness and love. These prayers are the equivalent of the preacher telling the same story three times but with the same ending. Florence, Gabriel, and Elizabeth—this unholy trinity—are frustrated in their quest for salvation.

The overarching sermonic vision of heroic struggle and overcoming is given full expression in John's walking through the white fire of the threshing floor. "The thrust of the sermon," Spillers notes, "is passional, repeating essentially the rhythms of plot, complication, climax, resolution. The sermon is an oral poetry—not simply an exegetical, theological presentation, but a complete expression of a gamut of emotions whose central form is the narrative and whose end is cathartic release. In that regard the sermon is an instrument of a collective catharsis, binding once again the isolated members of community."[8]

In terms of narrative structure, part 1, "The Seventh Day," establishes the mood and introduces the theme, which is the power of

6. "Fabrics of History," 29.
7. LeRoi Jones, *Blues People*, 17–31, and Wendall Whalum, "Black Hymnody," 341–55.
8. Spillers, "Fabrics of History," 4.

redemptive love. Part 2, "The Prayers of the Saints," a series of prayers/confessions, functions as the equivalent of the chorus (the response); that is, the prayers/confessions are comments on John's questions (the call), but he is cut off from the historical past that influences the attitude of both his father and his mother toward him. Metaphorically, the blending of voices in part 3, "The Threshing Floor," offers the power of redemptive love as the resolution to the impasse between father and son. The conflict, rooted in slavery, centers on Gabriel's blocking John's route to manhood; and, ostensibly, Gabriel forecloses the possibility of the power of redemptive love. John is ignorant of the fact that he is a bastard. Equally important, "The Threshing Floor" as metaphor represents the slave past with which black people must come to terms. This terrible burden of history threatens to rip the Grimes family apart. It serves as an ironic counterstatement to Gabriel's favorite scripture: "Set thine house in order, for thou shalt die and not live" (Isa. 38:1).

Try as he might, Gabriel, who embodies the classic sermonic vision of the fall, cannot set his house in order until he confronts his past. Grounded in a rigid black puritanism, Gabriel is the rebellious angel, and the repercussions from his fall prove injurious to everyone who is dear to him—his mother, his sister, his two wives, and especially his stepson John. Gabriel's fall is precipitated by his insincere promises, arrogance, and history. Down South, he had held the key to his family's freedom from blinding poverty; up North, he holds fast to his prominence as a church man to hide from his previous transgressions, but the church position neither protects his family from poverty nor elevates him to a state of grace. Overwhelmed by his family's powerlessness and abject poverty, Gabriel seeks relief in riotous living from a future foreclosed by enforced segregation. The more his mother prays for him to repent, or, as the folk say, "to get right with God," the more determinedly he runs headlong toward self-destruction.

Resentful of her brother's privileged position, Florence deserts her family and moves north, leaving a decadent Gabriel to care for their mother. Shocked into being responsible by her bold act, Gabriel undergoes a religious conversion, becomes a preacher, and marries Deborah, who has been raped. The black, bony, and barren Deborah becomes too heavy a cross for a chastened Gabriel to bear; he backslides and has a torrid nine-day affair with his attractive fellow household servant Esther. Their affair produces a son, Royal, whom he disowns.

Gabriel's life has been marked by his fear of fathering an ill-conceived line. Even in the midst of his decadence, this prodigal son wants "power . . . to be the Lord's anointed" (94). It weighs heavily upon his conscience that he may die a sinner and not leave any legitimate offspring: "Thus, when he came to the harlot, he came to her in rage, and he left her in vain sorrow—feeling himself to have been, once more, most foully robbed, having spent his holy seed in a forbidden darkness where it could only die" (95). The one constant in his life is his desire to father a holy line. The vision of being a blessed patriarch leads him to circumvent the moral integrity of his mother's religion, which thrives on inclusion, not exclusion. As if to mock his own vision, he sires two roguish sons, Royal and Roy. In short, his rage stems from his awareness that the much-praised John is not made in his own image.

Now, in his present reflection, Gabriel can find little in which to rejoice. This study in defeated hope is driven into the sanctuary of the church to gain a measure of dignity and identity. However, Gabriel derives none of the residual benefits of black worship—the camaraderie and fellowship. The unsympathetic narrator refers to him, somewhat mockingly, as "a kind of fill-in speaker, a holy handyman" (51). Gabriel is an example of those church-going individuals who have harmony in their throats but do not have the Holy Ghost in their hearts. In fairness, it should be pointed out that Gabriel has some redeeming qualities: he comforts his mother on her deathbed (returning to the scene of his desertion after leaving an embittered Florence to care for her), defends Deborah against the jibes and jokes of the other "holy men," and, apart from his nine-day affair with Esther, he remains faithful to Deborah during their eighteen-year marriage. Unlike his father, Gabriel does not desert his wife, Elizabeth. He struggles to support and protect his family. The reader, therefore, can sympathize with and understand him even while he or she, with John, wants to hate him.[9]

The socially licensed role of preacher provides Gabriel with an acceptable route out of a highly untenable situation. This built-in forum confers a certain amount of prominence and respect on this

9. Allen, "Religious Symbolism," 195.

semiliterate peasant. One hears the sonorous voice of black preachers such as John Jasper (immortalized in Johnson's *God's Trombones*) in Baldwin's lavish description of Gabriel's conversion at that rapturous moment when man and God commune:[10]

> "Then," he testified, "I heard my mother singing. She was a-singing for me. She was a-singing low and sweet, right there beside me, like she knew if she just called Him, the Lord would come." When he heard this singing, which filled all the silent air, which swelled until it filled all the waiting earth, the heart within him broke, and yet began to rise, lifted of its burden; and his throat unlocked; and his tears came down as though the listening skies had opened. "Then I praised God, Who had brought me out of Egypt and set my feet on the solid rock." When at last he lifted up his eyes he saw a new Heaven and a new earth; and he heard a new sound of singing, for a sinner had come home. "I looked at my hands and my hands were new. And I opened my mouth to the Lord that day and Hell won't make me change my mind." And, yes, there was singing everywhere; the birds and the crickets and the frogs rejoiced, the distant dogs leaping and sobbing, circled in their narrow yards, and roosters cried from every high fence that here was a new beginning, a blood-washed day! (97)

In Gabriel's conversion scene, Baldwin invokes deeply ingrained mascons such as "swing low, sweet chariot" and "let my people go," which stress the linkage between black suffering and the Israelites in Egyptian bondage. Baldwin then shows that all nature bears witness to Gabriel's conversion, indicating its cosmological significance. But Gabriel's apocalyptic vision serves in later years only to intensify his sense of frustrated redemption; consequently, he stands ready to block John from experiencing this newness in Christ, that is, from sharing in the joy and agony of celebration.

Gabriel preaches with such fire and conviction that he is invited to preach at the Twenty-Four Elders Revival Meeting. This "monster revival meeting [attracted] evangelists from all the surrounding counties, from as far south as Florida and as far north as Chicago" (100). Gabriel takes Isaiah 6:5 as the text for his sermon: "Then said I, Woe is me! for I am undone; because I am a man of

10. For a portrait of John Jasper (1812–1901), whose fame was based largely on his simple, ungrammatical language, imagery, and emotionalism, see William E. Hatcher, *John Jasper: The Unmatched Negro Philosopher and Preacher.* For a more balanced portrait of Jasper, see Spillers, "Fabrics of History," 83–139.

unclean lips, and I dwell in the midst of a people of unclean lips: for mine eyes have seen the King, the Lord of Hosts." Still a youth in Christ, Gabriel uses Isaiah's original call to the prophetic ministry to place a theological punctuation mark on the end of his decadent lifestyle. Like Isaiah, Gabriel pronounces the prophetic *Woe* upon himself. Thus, his grand gesture to a distinguished group of "war horses" (101) was a statement of total self-condemnation: "I am undone. . . . I am a man of unclean lips." Before the holy God, sinful man cannot stand.

Cleansed by God's forgiving act, Gabriel invokes Isaiah's consecration and embarks on the great preaching mission that he feels confident will define his career. Gabriel's confession of his personal sin bought the response of God's cleansing to equip him for service to the Lord (Isa. 6:6–8). The altar is the place of blood sacrifice, or the place of expiation or intercession. (When John lies on the threshing floor in need of an intercessor, we see how Gabriel is ironically judged by the words of this sermon, as well as by others.) Gabriel's sermon earns him considerable praise, though he is quick to undercut this praise by chastening his Elders for their unkind remarks directed at the degraded Deborah during the sumptuous dinner. Even here, the exhortations of the sanctimonious Gabriel ring false.

Baldwin recontextualizes the familiar allegory of the church depicted as the bride of Christ (Rev. 19) when the Twenty-Four Elders gather "in the upper room of the lodge hall [for] the spectacular dinner that was to end the revival" (106). Just as the Seer in Revelation describes a new relation between God and his people as a marriage, Gabriel ascends the stairs expecting to enter into a new relationship with the Elders. The banquet is to cement his position in the ministry. Gabriel's expectations are dashed (as we shall see). The entrance of God into his eternal reign and the marriage of Christ and the church "are parallel ways of expressing the same grounds for joy and exultation."[11]

The defeat of the spiritual Babylon (see Rev. 18) causes the throng of people in heaven to burst into joyful celebration again. They praise God for his salvation, his glory, his honor, his power, and his victory over the "great prostitute" (Rev. 19.2 New International Version), who was responsible for the deaths of the believing martyrs.

11. MacLean, "The Revelation to John," 965.

Then the twenty-four elders (probably representing all the Christian martyrs in heaven) and the four living creatures (probably an order of angelic beings whose task is to guard the heavenly throne and lead in worship of God) shout in antiphonal response to the praises of the multitude, which Gabriel fervently desires and which is denied.

The twenty-four elders are a palpable manifestation of the intimate relationship between God and his people. Through Jesus, "the Lamb"—the unity meal in the Upper Room signifies the ultimate joining together of Christ and his church—the people he has redeemed with his own blood are saved. Because of the cleansing power of the blood of the Lamb, the church is arrayed in "fine linen, bright and clean" (Rev. 19:8). Thus the church is ready to be united with Christ. Just as the self-righteous Gabriel, "a new man in Christ Jesus" (99), cannot overlook a sexually offensive remark at the unity supper, contemptuously seeing his esteemed colleagues as "highly paid circus-performers" (107), he cannot forgive Elizabeth for her transgression. His heart refuses to yield, to forgive, and to embrace John as his own, but he expects Jesus, the Lamb of God, to forgive him his transgressions. Gabriel's life is guided by torment and sorrow, which form the recapitulative subtext for Baldwin's Calvinistic discourse on sin and redemption.

Gabriel's two dreams point up the extremes of his position. The first, a wet dream, signifies to him the world, flesh, devil that he must battle if he is to walk with the saints. The other dream, of climbing a high mountain and attaining a peaceful field from which "the elect" are seen toiling upward, represents to him a promise.[12] "So shall thy seed be" (112), a voice says as he wakes. With his marriage to Deborah, though well intentioned, he denies the needs of the flesh that influence his future course of action. Yet he cannot realize his goal of being the Lord's anointed, a patriarch, like Abraham. Gabriel's sin is not just in his actions but in what he fails to do. He asks the Lord's forgiveness for his sins while he is unwilling to forgive the sins of others: Florence's desertion, leaving him to care for their sick mother; Deborah, his dead first wife, because she was barren and sexless; Elizabeth, for having a child out of wedlock; and John, for being the son of the bondwoman and not his rightful heir.

12. Sylvander, *James Baldwin*, 32.

Gabriel represents the religious sense of being a hypocrite. He is trapped in his personal history of deceit and denial, which he does not acknowledge. This makes him a unique character in black American literature, where blacks are ordinarily trapped in the collected history of the race. The repetitious nature of an oppressive history is for them a constant reminder of their former status as slaves; the quality of their lives does not reflect significant material improvement. By and large, the culturally sanctioned American Dream is off limits to them. Consequently, many blacks, seeking release from the continual oppression, spend a disproportionate amount of their energy in antisocial behavior (e.g., drug and alcohol abuse). They also seek release through inspirational religion that challenges "the bourgeois character of the mainline Black denominations and the racist posture of the White churches."[13]

The hypocritical Gabriel embodies a religious worldview that is pejoratively referred to as "pie-in-the-sky." He moves from the past to the future; he will not claim the present. For him the apocalypse—the kingdom of God—has arrived, but for no one else in his family. From his self-righteous position, he sees John as the devil and Elizabeth as a fallen woman. Ironically, Roy, the remnant of the holy line, turns out to be the demon. In essence, Gabriel is not only at war with the Christian ethos that one should own his or her history (schematized as the blackness of sin) and seek forgiveness, but he is also at war with his cultural heritage. The concrete manifestation of this is his inability to successfully evoke the culturally embedded vision of striving and overcoming in his sermons. Blocked at every turn, this "holy handyman" takes out his frustrations on his family.

It should come as no surprise that John equates Gabriel's authoritarian reign of theological terror with a vengeful God—"an equivalent, incidentally, of the black view of whiteness implicit in this novel."[14] Ironically, the more Gabriel wraps himself in the bosom of the church, the more he disregards the moral integrity of his mother's religion, inclusion over exclusion. During a church service, the black preacher expresses this idea when he warmly says, "Everybody is a child of God."

13. Wilmore, *Black Religion and Black Radicalism,* 210; E. Franklin Frazier, "The Failure of the Negro Intellectual," 52–66. See also Hans A. Baer, *The Black Spiritual Movement: A Religious Response to Racism,* 3–30.

14. Stanley Macebuh, *James Baldwin: A Critical Study,* 53.

Visible People, Invisible Religion

The Grimes family actively supports the Temple of the Fire Baptized. "It was not the biggest church in Harlem, nor yet the smallest, but John had been brought up to believe it was the holiest and the best" (12). Its lower-class members who work as domestics and factory workers are transformed—in the charged religious atmosphere—from the drudgery of invisible workers into saints who rejoice in praising the Lord (Deacons and Bishops and Sisters and Brothers). The sanctimonious Gabriel typifies the church membership. These migrants to the industrial city live in overcrowded tenements and work in dead-end jobs, so they engage in ecstatic worship services to take some of the hurt out of their shattered dreams. To be sure, their frustrations speak to modern man's use of religion to negate his spiritual rootlessness in industrial society.

In *The Black Church since Frazier,* C. Eric Lincoln outlines the signal importance of the black church in a rigidly segregated society. It is the "spiritual face of the black community. . . . Because of the peculiar nature of the Black experience and the centrality of institutionalized religion in the development of that experience, the time was when the personal dignity of the Black individual was communicated almost entirely through his church affiliation." To be able to say "I belong to the Temple of the Fire Baptized" was the accepted way of establishing identity and status when there were few other criteria by means of which a sense of self or a communication of place could be projected. In effect, "the social identity of the Black-american as well as his self-perception," Lincoln continues, "are still to an important degree refracted through the prism of his religious identity."[15]

The members of the Temple of the Fire Baptized have the usual self-contradictory combination of strengths and weaknesses and of good and bad qualities regularly to be discovered among people everywhere. This is the backdrop of the social pressures brought to bear upon the consciousness of the fourteen-year-old John Grimes

15. *The Black Church since Frazier,* 115–16. For other commentators on the church being as a refuge and as a source of strength for these weary travelers in the urban North, see Drake and Cayton, *Black Metropolis;* Arthur E. Paris, *Black Pentecostalism: Southern Religion in an Urban World;* and Hans A. Baer, *The Black Spiritual Movement: A Religious Response to Racism.*

as he stands before the bar of his community. Unlike Roy, his wild brother, John is expected to be a preacher.

To Gabriel's everlasting consternation, John, "the son of the bondwoman, stood where the rightful heir should stand" (114). In spite of his promise to Elizabeth prior to their marriage that he would love the child John as if he were his own son, Gabriel, his heart grown heavy with a vindictive rage, rejects the love of his obedient stepson John. Gabriel's life shows that men are free to do what they choose, but they cannot control the consequences of their choices. This self-righteous man expects everyone to bow down before him. These are the as yet unarticulated tensions that John wonders about on his fourteenth birthday. Most of all, he wonders about his relation to his father, whom he so desperately wants to please. In this context, his life serves a ritual purpose in that it embodies the sermonic vision of heroic struggle and overcoming and black America's longing to be accepted by white America.

John must come to terms with his father's rejection and transcend that rejection by surrendering himself to the redemptive power of God's love. This is considerable cause for anguish, as John has difficulty in separating his religiously rigid, authoritarian father from a terrorizing God:

> His father's arm, rising and falling, might make him cry, and that voice might cause him to tremble; yet his father could never be entirely the victor, for John cherished something that his father could not reach. It was his hatred and his intelligence that he cherished, the one feeding the other. He lived for the day when his father would be dying and he, John, would curse him on his deathbed. . . . John's heart was hardened against the Lord. His father was God's minister, the ambassador of the King of Heaven, and John could not bow before the throne of grace without first kneeling to his father. On his refusal to do this had his life depended, and John's secret heart had flourished in its wickedness until the day his sin first covered him. (20–21)

John uses his intelligence as a weapon in his implacable struggle with his self-righteous father. His mind becomes a safe harbor to escape momentarily from Gabriel's reign of "theological terror." His refusal to bow before his father prevents John from experiencing the religious ecstasy that he has observed on the radiant faces of the saints. On his fourteenth birthday, John feels the pressure to bow before God—symbolized by the threshing floor—and be admitted into the community of saints. Before he can be admitted, the rebellious John must conquer his hatred for his father and his unbelief and scorn for God. Because he sees no acceptable route to deliverance, his fear of both is intensified. John needs an intercessor other than his father, who, he feels, has robbed the religious experience of its joy and ecstasy. The svelte Elisha is the mediator who joins subject and object.[16]

In contrast to the reserved and studious John, the brash Elisha is charismatic, handsome, and sensual. Unlike John, he is comfortable with the church as the route to salvation. He sees no contradiction between his manliness and surrendering himself to God. Nevertheless, in regard to outlets for affirmative and creative self-expression, John and Elisha mirror each other in their bleak surroundings, with the distinction being that Elisha is much more comfortable with his sexuality.

By depicting John's steamy wrestling match with Elisha beneath the altar, Baldwin forces the reader to confront the church as a site that is instrumental in the formation of sexual identity. For example, until John resolves his theological limbo, he will remain ambivalent about his sexual identity, compounded by his father's constant demeaning of his masculinity. The overarching question for John is: does my heavenly Father accept me just as I am?

Moreover, Baldwin subtly suggests that black men must early in their lives rein in their ambitions or be dealt with harshly by a hostile white society that is threatened by their unbowed sexuality. The religious arena provides a segment of black men with a socially acceptable outlet for their awakening sexuality and circumscribed ambitions. We come to realize that the wrestling scene foreshadows John's writhing on the threshing floor as he undergoes the agony and the ecstasy of the religious shock.

Elisha's "shout" prefigures this electric moment. It represents the apotheosis of the ecstatic dimension of black religion, with its com-

16. Macebuh, *James Baldwin*, 53. Elijah found Elisha, a prosperous farmer's son, plowing and appointed him to be his successor. Elisha also became a great prophet of the ninth century B.C., performing many miracles and acting as counselor to several kings. When Elisha saw Elijah ascend in a chariot of fire into heaven, he cried, "My father, my father, the chariot of Israel, and the horsemen thereof." See 1 Kings 19:16–21 and 2 Kings 2:4–9, 13.

bination of agony and joy. Dripping with sensuality, the tall, athletic Elisha pulls all eyes toward his angular body:

> At one moment, head thrown back, eyes closed, sweat standing on his brow, [Elisha] sat at the piano, singing and playing; and then, like a great, black cat in trouble in the jungle, he stiffened and trembled, and cried out. *Jesus, Jesus, oh Lord Jesus!* He struck on the piano one last, wild note, and threw up his hands, palms upward, stretched wide apart. The tambourines raced to fill the vacuum left by his silent piano, and his cry drew answering cries. Then he was on his feet, turning, blind, his face congested, contorted with this rage, and the muscles leaping and swelling in his long, dark neck. It seemed that he could not breathe, that his body could not contain this passion, that he would be, before their eyes, dispersed into the waiting air. His hands, rigid to the very fingertips, moved outward and back against his hips, his sightless eyes looked upward, and he began to dance. Then his hands closed into fists, and his head snapped downward, his sweat loosening the grease that slicked down his hair; and the rhythm of all the others quickened to match Elisha's rhythm; his thighs moved terribly against the cloth of his suit, his heels beat on the floor, and his fists moved beside his body as though he were beating his own drum. (15–16)

In this passage, Baldwin reaches a crescendo of black sermonic style in his unparalleled description of the shout and its effect on the aesthetic community. Like a black preacher, he uses a variety of oratorical techniques: alliteration, repetition, parallelism, metaphors. In addition, the short, staccato sentences reproduce the surging rhythms in the sermon-like prose. One hears the preacher sucking in air between the rapid-fire sentences, feels the energy and vitality that is unleashed, and senses the drama that places one squarely in the center of the action. With its steaming sensuality, Elisha's holy dance adds to the drama as he must come to grips with the needs of the flesh as well as the demands of his fundamentalist religion. Baldwin deftly shows the reader the overdetermined source of the religious imagination in the black community. Disbarred from the American Dream, many in black America seek refuge and release from the troubles of the world behind the closed doors of their churches.

Inherent in Elisha's shout is what Baldwin in *Notes of a Native Son* refers to as "the rage of the disesteemed." This rage powers the rejoicing saints: "Their singing caused [John] to believe in the presence of the Lord. . . . he could not doubt that it was, for them, the very bread of life. . . . it was as though wherever they might be became the upper room, and the Holy Ghost were riding on the air" (14–15). The shout as "performance event" is ritual representation of black people's quest to break free from the physical and psychological chains that bind them in a state of perpetual inferiority. Gerald L. Davis observes that this "metaphonic performance" invites the audience to "break free" of their day-to-day constraints and lose themselves in the most emotionally charged mascon, *Jesus, Jesus, oh Lord Jesus!* Elisha's performance carries cosmological weight in that it is intrinsically embedded in the day-to-day lives of the people. Elisha's sensuality is the outward manifestation of a sense of life that does not exclude joy from worship.[17] Structurally, this scene prepares the reader for John's experience on the threshing floor.

In many respects, the dead mother remains the central figure in the lives of Florence and Gabriel. This spiritual figure guided her family during the dark days of Reconstruction. When Florence on bended knees and with bowed head prays, she remembers her mother's fervent prayer to God to protect her family from the night-riders:

> Dear Father, . . . we come before You on our knees this evening to ask you to watch over us and hold back the hand of the destroying angel. Lord, sprinkle the doorpost of this house with the blood of the Lamb to keep all the wicked men away. Lord, we praying for every mother's son and daughter everywhere in the world but we want You to take special care of this girl here tonight, Lord, and don't let no evil come nigh her. We know You's able to do it, Lord, in Jesus' name, Amen. (68)

The chiseled simplicity of the mother's prayer touches the black experience at its core; its beautiful scriptural rhythms reveal the moral integrity of a faith tested by fire. Her redemptive vision stands in sharp contrast to Gabriel's use of religion to suffocate man's communion with God. Her prayer begins with a complimentary salutation to the Almighty, immediately followed by stock phrases and formulaic expressions ("on our knees this evening")

17. Baldwin, *Notes of a Native Son*, 165, and Davis, *I Got the World in Me*, 29.

that call attention to the setting. She asks the Lord to "hold back the hand of the destroying angel," a finely wrought metaphor that refers to the white men who are terrorizing the defenseless black community. "The destroying angel" is a trope relating to the Passover, when the Lord avenged himself on the Egyptians for Pharaoh's killing of the Israelite male children.

This inversion enables the mother to unleash her jeremiadic call for revenge and redemption: "Lord, sprinkle the doorpost of this house with the blood of the Lamb to keep all the wicked men away." The highly imagistic language in this short prayer supports Hurston's observation that "in the mouth of the Negro the English language loses its stiffness, yet conveys its meaning accurately."[18] For example, the phrase "hold back the hand of the destroying angel" conveys just as accurate a picture of imminent destruction as if Baldwin had written something like "the dance of death in the eyes of white men."

And finally, the mother's prayer is a study in sermonic genealogy. By *genealogy,* I mean that it links the past with the present to form a critical biography that accounts for the tensions in the father-son relationship. The mother fervently prays for "a community where love and justice would prevail."[19] She emphasizes the communal, not the individual. By way of comparison, Gabriel corrupts his mother's religion. He sanctimoniously uses it as a tool to create theological terror in his household. The embittered Florence is keenly aware of Gabriel's self-righteous attitude when she kneels to pray. "She knew that Gabriel rejoiced, not that her humility might lead her to grace, but only that some private anguish had brought her low" (65). It should be pointed out that Florence, in some respects, once stood in the same relation to her mother as John does to Gabriel.

Five years Gabriel's senior, Florence, the dutiful, intellectually inclined daughter, takes a back seat ("her future was swallowed up" [72]) to the man-child, as all must be sacrificed for him. Gabriel, the wayward son, rewards his mother for her efforts on his behalf and for her placing Florence in a secondary position with drink and debauchery, decadence and riotous living. Meanwhile,

18. *Sanctified Church,* 81.
19. Moyd, *Redemption in Black Theology,* 16.

Florence, whose anger turns inward, is justifiably embittered. Florence becomes the blues to Gabriel's attempted spiritual. His inability to accept people as they are blinds him to the fact that salvation is an ongoing process, not an event, that today's disappointment may provide the impetus for tomorrow's triumph. Ironically, Florence, who knows Gabriel's sordid history, is able to separate the sacred from the profane without undue psychological damage. Of the two, she emerges as the more wholesome.

Baldwin blends two narrative streams in *Go Tell:* the blues and the spiritual. The correspondence between the blues and the spiritual streams, flowing from the same soil, is taken as a matter of course in terms of the sermon. Florence represents the former, unrepentant and still embittered over her lot in life: the education of her brother placed above hers, the "victimization of women at the hands of men," and intragroup color discrimination.[20] Elizabeth represents the latter—the spiritual. The church is her life, to put up with Gabriel's temper tantrums, domestic violence, and the rejection of her son, the one whom he promised to love and cherish as his own.

Gabriel stands in both traditions. He sins in the flesh, which in turn drives him into the church; yet, paradoxically, Gabriel's sins of the flesh deny him "true" prominence in the church—he who so desperately seeks a sign from God. This can be seen as a double, self-enfolding irony when one considers the majesty and awe associated with his name. His angelic namesake was entrusted with perhaps the most awesome responsibility in the Bible, literally and figuratively to blow the trumpet on Judgment Day—to go tell *it,* that Judgment Day is at hand. Ironically, Gabriel Grimes sits in judgment on his bastard stepson, John, who by his daily good deeds, diligence, and acts of kindness reminds Gabriel of his past transgressions, which deny him the keys to the kingdom. The magnitude of Gabriel's personal corruption extends even to the dust that seeps into his house:

> Dirt was in every corner, angle, crevice of the monstrous stove, and lived behind it in delirious communion with the corrupted

20. Trudier Harris, *Black Women in the Fiction of James Baldwin,* 20. Harris observes that the women in Baldwin's *Go Tell* "are all limited in the emotional relationships they form with the men in their lives" (13). She argues that we should see the limitations of the women within the context of the fundamentalist church in the black community that defines their lives.

> wall. Dirt was in the baseboard that John scrubbed every Saturday, and roughened the cupboard shelves that held the cracked and gleaming dishes. Under this dark weight the walls leaned, under it the ceiling, with a great crack like lightening in its center, sagged. The windows gleamed like beaten gold or silver, but now John saw, in the yellow light, how fine dust veiled their doubtful glory. (22)

This is the burden of history that weighs so heavily on Gabriel's shoulders and perhaps explains his rather skeptical attitude in regard to John's conversion. Gabriel's rejection of his bastard stepson is a metaphor for white America's rejection of black America.

Baldwin in the climactic "The Threshing Floor" creates an atmosphere of autobiographical authenticity in his depiction of black inspirational worship. He invokes the "grammar of emotion" as he brings together the various archetypes, motifs, and religious symbols. The felicitous figurative language and concrete details are not mere background, offering only atmosphere for the action; they invariably become an integral part of the cultural biography of the community. John's conversion is the rite of passage from a sheltered life to an infinitely more complex one. His "going through" represents the apotheosis of the spiritual moment in African American expression. The church provides him with a language so that he may be able to answer the autobiographical questions about which he wonders on the morning of his fourteenth birthday: Who am I? Does God love me? In the process of going through, John Grimes writes over the negative meaning of his surname—allegedly indicative of his corrupted state—as he breaks free of a constraining subjectivity in which the dominant culture asserts that he (and by extension the black community) sees only the back and not the face of God.

Thus the central issue is not that John lives in a world in which he cannot visualize a primordial structure; the issue is how to surrender the self to that structure. The impotent corporate community, therefore, privileges the unseen as it overcompensates for its inability to make the world in its own image, to texturize the world. As a socially authorized forum that overrides this historical impotence, the black church, as a central component of African American discourse where personae, protagonist, and the latent autobiographical voice come together, enables the corporate community to *re-cognize* itself and achieves what Houston A. Baker refers to as "a resonant, improvisational, expressive dignity."[21]

Preparation for the *cognition* and *re-cognition* begins with the devotional service that concludes part 1. The devotional service activates the latent cultural values and sets in motion the ritual forces that lead to the penultimate moment, John's conversion—his walking "through that white fire" (66)—in part 3. The devotional service recalls the "prayer meeting" or "praise house" of the plantation, the place where blacks felt they could express themselves as freely and emotionally as possible. LeRoi Jones in *Blues People* informs us that central to the praise house was the African dictum: "The Spirit will not descend without music."[22]

Thus, Sister McCandless formally calls the saints to order with song: "I reckon we might have a little song . . . just to warm things up. I sure hate to walk in a church where folks is just sitting and talking. Look like it takes all my spirit away" (59). The music feeds the emotions and the emotions feed the music. "Then," John observes, "the church seemed to swell with the Power it held, and, like a planet rocking in space, the Temple rocked with the power of God" (15).

The continuous music, with percussive elements of hand-clapping and foot-stomping and shouting, generates tremendous social pressure for the sinner to come to God. Unlike Roy, John is under intense pressure to "go through," to redefine his relationship with family and community, and to claim his relationship to God. From this perspective, the music of black preaching—which is a constant during John's going through—can be understood as a sort of "singing in the spirit," for there is a surplus (*glossa*) expressed in the music that accompanies the rational content (*logos*) enunciated in words.

As a "church of emotion," Jones observes, "the Afro-Christian church is informed by the call and response which shapes the worship service." The call and response as a shaping influence on the worship service is nowhere more evident than in the storefront church. Founded as a protest church—a protest against the structure and strictures of the mainline denominational black churches—

21. *Blues, Ideology, and Afro-American Literature,* 13.

22. *Blues People,* 40–41. See also Fauset, *Black Gods of the Metropolis,* 76–86; Eileen Southern, *The Music of Black Americans,* 212–14; and Paris, *Black Pentecostalism,* 61–71.

the storefront churches nevertheless have in common with their denominational brothers a core of elements: preaching, praying, singing, and testifying, overlaid with African-based rhythms.[23] The storefront churches are also caught up in the balkanization of Christianity. For example, the Water Baptized become members in the body of Christ by immersion, while the Temple of the Fire Baptized become members in the body of Christ by successfully "going through" on the threshing floor.

Biblical farmers cut grain in the field and bound it into sheaves, which were then transported to the threshing floor, a smooth, round plot of ground. There the grain was threshed in order to remove the grain from the ears. Threshing was done either by beating out the grain by hand using a threshing sledge (a sled with teeth to separate the grain from the straw) or with the use of oxen to tread the grain on the threshing floor (Deut. 25:4). As the grain was threshed, it sank through the straw and the straw was crushed into tiny pieces.

The mixture was then winnowed, a process that used a wooden fork or shovel, called a fan, to toss the grain, straw, and chaff into the air, normally during the evening breeze. The wind would separate the material by blowing the light straw into a heap and the lighter chaff and dust still further. Only the grain would fall back to the floor. The chaff was then burned and the straw used as animal feed. The grain was gathered into the barn. Thus the biblical writers would refer to this process to emphasize God's separation of the righteous from the ungodly.[24]

Baldwin uses John Grimes as a symbol to illustrate how a community reconstitutes its fractured soul by using Christianity as a mode of coming to terms with its place in the universe. John, by going through on the threshing floor, is the community's representative, a mirror of their lives, actively engaged in a celebratory ritual of confession and cleansing. By admitting to their failures, John and the enraptured community admit to the simultaneous absurdity and beauty of life.

Like the preacher, Baldwin begins slowly and then builds the sermonic structure of his narrative to an emotional pitch that ends in the climactic scene with John on the threshing floor. A correspon-

23. Jones, *Blues People,* 41–48.

24. Cf. Ps. 1:4, Isa. 41:15–16, Matt. 3:12, and Luke 3:17. See also Fred Wright, *Manners and Culture of Bible Lands.*

dence exists between the call and response and the alternating focus on John's spiritual progress in between the flashbacks of the prostrate sinners. Where the preacher in the call and response enthusiastically asks the congregation, "Have you got good religion?" and they respond, "Certainly, Lord," Baldwin frames his sermon around John's question "How can I make my father love me?" and Elisha's impassioned charge "Go through, go through!"

To go through, John must first resolve the darkness of his sin: "The darkness of his sin was in the hardheartedness with which he resisted God's power; in the scorn that was often his while he listened to the crying, breaking voices, and watched the black skin glisten while they lifted up their arms and fell on their faces before the Lord. For he had made his decision. He would not be like his father, or his father's fathers. He would have another life" (19).

Macebuh reminds us that the God John sets himself in opposition to "in the darkness of his sin" is "ultimately an abstraction against which rebellion can at best be fanciful" and that, for all intents and purposes, that God is really Gabriel, "who in many significant respects *is* God [and] becomes the actual and visible objects of John's fear and hatred."[25] The fear and hatred that John has for his father is revealed in the bathtub scene:

> Yes, he had sinned: one morning, alone, in the dirty bathroom, the square, dirt-gray cupboard room that was filled with the stink of his father. Sometimes, leaning over the cracked, "tattle-tale gray" bathtub, he scrubbed his father's back; and looked, as the accursed son of Noah had looked, on his father's hideous nakedness. It was secret, like sin, and slimy, like the serpent, and heavy, like the rod. Then he hated his father, and longed for the power to cut his father down. (197)

In this passage, Baldwin brings together the main points of tension in the narrative: (1) Abraham and the covenant, (2) the Hamitic myth, and (3) the Ishmael-Isaac-Jacob discord. Baldwin uses the father-son conflict embedded in the Freudian Oedipus complex to make clever adaptations of biblical analogues. Baldwin presents the tension in this father-son conflict in archetypal patterns in order to emphasize the universal aspect of their conflict.[26]

25. *James Baldwin*, 53.

26. Though a great many sources were involved in my thinking on how Baldwin

Baldwin established links between God's covenant with Abraham and Gabriel's vision in the novel's opening pages. Gabriel, who longs to be the Lord's anointed, desires to hold the covenant like Abraham on behalf of the tribe and pass this power to his son with his blessing. "Gabriel has spiritual as well as temporal authority, so John must kneel to his father before he can kneel to the Lord."[27] The tension grows out of John's recognition of the objective reality. It is "his father's church" as well as "his father's house," and John's rebellion against him includes rebellion against the whole race: "He would not be like his father, or his father's fathers" (19). In a double play on the Hebrew story, the father looks to enter into a covenantal relationship with God while the son identifies with the Israelites longing for freedom from Egyptian bondage.

As Gabriel inventories his life from his position as supplicant, he makes it clear before his conversion that he wants to become "the Lord's anointed" and not die in a state of sin that would deny him the promise of an heir. Correspondingly, Gabriel's first important sermon engages the issue of sexual sin and paternity. It is based on a text from St. Paul: "And if ye be Christ's, then ye are Abraham's seed, and heirs according to the promise" (104). He marries Deborah to "continue the line of the faithful, a royal line" (109) after waking up one night to find himself "covered with his own white seed" (111) and then dreaming that God called him to the top of a mountain, showed him the elect, and promised (in the words of the Lord to Abraham), "So shall thy seed be" (112). His reaction to Esther's pregnancy is horror that "the seed of the prophet would be nourished" in the womb of a harlot (129). In most religious earnestness he names his son with Elizabeth Roy (and Esther ironically names her son with him Royal) to preserve his symbolic identification with the kings of Israel—from Saul, who was anointed by the Lord, to Jesus, whose title is Christ, or Messiah, "the anointed One."

For Gabriel, salvation is connected with lawful paternity. When

---

brings together the main points of tension in *Go Tell*, the principal source involved in my discussion at this point is Allen's "Religious Symbolism and Psychic Reality in Baldwin's *Go Tell It on the Mountain*," 173–99. Allen delineates the scriptural basis for the father-son conflict fueled by Gabriel's obsessive desire to maintain the purity of the line of patriarchal succession and the latent sexual overtones that enliven the conflict.

27. Allen, "Religious Symbolism," 194.

Roy calls him a bastard, he considers it a curse (114). For this reason, Gabriel's hatred of John is twofold: first, because the "son of the bondwoman" might stand in the place of "the rightful heir"; and second, because Elizabeth, mother of the prophet, might have contaminated Roy by not thoroughly repenting the conception of John. In Gabriel's eyes, John is cursed before he is born; therefore, he has no opportunity for redemption. The covenant theme expresses Gabriel's psychological motivation—his thirst for power and his feelings of sexual guilt—and this theme is reflected in his behavior toward Deborah, Esther, Elizabeth, Roy, and John. Through the symbolic identification with Abraham, we understand Gabriel.

Overcome with guilt as a result of his fall into sin with Esther, Gabriel preaches in distant communities as penance for this infidelity to Deborah. His three months as an itinerant preacher open his eyes to exploitation on a large scale. Gabriel sees how white oppression has driven blacks away from the Lord, how they have descended into a state of spiritual lawlessness in the wilderness of lechery, gambling, drinking, and jazz:

> There seemed . . . no woman . . . who had not seen her father, her brother, her lover, or her son cut down without mercy; who had not seen her sister become part of the white man's great whorehouse; . . . no man whose manhood had not been, at the root, sickened, whose loins had not been dishonored, whose seed had not been scattered into oblivion . . . into living shame and rage, and into endless battle. Yes, their parts were all cut off, they were dishonored, their very names were nothing more than dust blown disdainfully across the field of time—to fall where, to blossom where, bringing forth what fruit hereafter, where?—their very names were not their own. Behind them was the darkness, nothing but the darkness, and all around them destruction, and before them nothing but the fire—a bastard people, far from God, singing and crying in the wilderness! (137)

In the face of black impotence to combat white oppression, Gabriel's proud but broken-hearted mother had seen her children sold and Deborah raped and mutilated, an act that just as easily could have happened to Florence. Elizabeth's mother and father were both "part of the white man's great whorehouse." Her Richard, introspective and melancholy, was "cut down" by the white man. Black folk religion, therefore, is in large measure the response to this oppression. To achieve salvation, blacks must pay strict obedience to the law—the same law Gabriel twists for his own purpose. This explains why his mother established Gabriel in the covenant, to the extent of sacrificing Florence's education. It is no wonder that the mother cannot forgive Gabriel for his straying from the straight and narrow, nor that Gabriel breaks under this tremendous pressure. Are blacks doomed to live in a perpetual present and suffer the fate of Ham?

The Hamitic myth and the personal level of oppression and persecution are brought home to John in the bathtub scene (197). First John sees the relation of racial persecution to sexually based father-son hatred through the story of Noah and his son Ham. The novel's moral vision makes it very clear that John has every right to be fearful of sin as he is nurtured in this fundamentally rigid, evangelical Christian environment with its sense of personal corruption. John views his masturbation—the only serious sin of which he is conscious—as an almost unforgivable sin. By association of ideas he remembers that he, like Ham, has seen his father naked. Religious symbolism interprets the experience; the bathtub is dirty, suggesting sin, and his father's penis reminds him of the serpent and the rod, both symbols of Moses, the lawgiver. He recognizes the source of his "hate and understands Noah's reason for cursing Ham: sexual rivalry between the father-king and the son-subject—the Biblical parallel to the Oedipus situation."[28]

There is, however, another dimension to the father-son conflict. Baldwin cleverly inverts the Ishmael-Isaac-Jacob discord and presents it as a matter of perspective. The reader's sympathy is for John, who never suspects that Gabriel is not his real father. Gabriel sees the conflict in terms of Abraham and Ishmael when he thinks, "only the son of the bondwoman stood where the rightful heir should stand" (114). Earlier in the narrative, Gabriel uses as a text for one of his sermons Paul's translation of the story (epistle to the Galatians, 4:21–31) in an analogy to explain this difference between those bound by the law and the "children of the promise." To Gabriel, John is Ishmael, "born after the flesh"; he, therefore, must be exiled in order to protect the inheritance of the demon Roy, the true son of the promise, Isaac. The narrator uses the very religious faith

28. Ibid., 197.

that Gabriel professes first to convict him and second to show how he adapts scriptural paradigms to fit his own situation. A closer inspection reveals that John is not Ishmael, the eternal outsider, but Jacob, who supplanted his brother Esau as the accepted against the wishes of his father and with his mother's encouragement (Gen. 25:19–36:43).

Baldwin establishes the symbolic identification in part 1, where John is encouraged by his mother and Roy is clearly regarded by his father as the true heir. The overt symbolism is made manifest in the wrestling scene before the beginning of the Tarry Service. Before Jacob could claim the birthright, won on the human level by "buying" it from Esau and by tricking his father into giving it, he had to wrestle with the angel of the Lord. In a parallel action, on the night of his initiation into the community of saints, John wrestles with a strong and holy young man who represents the Lord.

A cursory reading of this playful scene suggests that Baldwin describes John's wrestling with Elisha in language that connotes the sexual and the sensual.[29] Baldwin, however, adds a layer of complexity as he represents John Grimes's biological/spiritual struggle on the threshing floor for what John and his aesthetic community believe it to be: nothing less than a true transformation. Baldwin has already prepared the reader for Elisha's role as John's guardian angel by giving some history of their friendship and by emphasizing Elisha's holiness.

More significantly, Baldwin identifies Elisha after the wrestling match as a "young man in the Lord; who, a priest after the order of Melchizedek, had been given power over death and Hell" (60)—recalling the words and messianic connotations of Ps. 110 and Heb. 7: 1–7. Appropriately, Elisha continues in his symbolic role as the angel of the Lord as John writhes on the threshing floor. His interposed body prevents Gabriel from striking John (150); his voice guides John through his medieval dread and fear of sin; and his parting kiss on John's forehead is called "the seal ineffaceable forever" (221), like the seal of God on the foreheads of the saved in Rev. 7:13–17:8.

29. Macebuh, *James Baldwin*, 53–61. Macebuh argues that John sees his standoff with Elisha as a manifestation of his power and is "filled with a wild delight" (53). To read the wrestling match only as an example of homosexual love is to rob the scene of the community's belief in the transformative power of the religious experience.

In the conversion, John is in search of definitive authentication of his really being a child of the God that he confronts. His father tells him he looks like the devil, and the neighborhood kids call him frog eyes. In other words, John wants to close the distance between himself and the implied protagonist (God) while expanding the distance between himself and his most explicit antagonist (Gabriel). He wants to move from outsider to insider in his desire to lessen the pain of his oppression, persecution, and alienation. To be sure, on a deeper level, John's trepidation, as Nathan Scott notes, speaks to man's deeper concern with "what is metaphysically problematic in human life."[30]

As he sees himself suspended above "the roaring, perhaps, of the fires of Hell" (196), John goes through the sinner's autobiography of despair:

> And he began to shout for help, seeing before him the lash, the fire, and the depthless water, seeing his head bowed down forever, he, John, the lowest among these lowly. And he looked for his mother, but her eyes were fixed on this dark army—she was claimed by this army. And his father would not help him, his father did not see him, and Roy lay dead.
>
> Then he whispered, not knowing that he whispered: "Oh, Lord, have mercy on me. Have mercy on me."
>
> And a voice, for the first time in all his terrible journey, spoke to John, through the rage and weeping, and fire, and darkness, and flood:
>
> "Yes," said the voice, "go through. Go through." (202)

Through the interaction of Elisha the preacher, John the unloved son takes the first traumatic steps toward his initiation into manhood—breaking free of the tyranny of an oppressive father and emerging with an enlarged sense of self. In order to have another life John must come to terms with the fact that God is not objective phenomena, as knowable as the composition of bricks in his tenement, but that God is an object of poetic contemplation, distinct and private for every individual.[31] John rises from the threshing floor as a changed man-child, ready for the tasks to be assigned him in the redemptive purpose of God.

30. "Judgment Marked by a Cellar: The American Negro Writer and the Dialectic of Despair," 22.

31. Spillers, "Fabrics of History," 71–74.

Central to the black sermonic vision is its capacity to celebrate the rise of the fallen man through heroic struggle and overcoming. In terms of sermonic form, Baldwin begins this process with the selection of a black spiritual as the title of his book:

> Go tell it on the mountain,
> Over the hills and everywhere,
> Go tell it on the mountain,
> That Jesus Christ is born.

The message of this Christmas song entails the spreading of the good news (the gospel) and refers to the message of Moses to the Pharaoh, "Let my people go." Thus John's apocalyptic vision looks back to the Old testament trials and tribulations of the Israelites and looks forward to the New Testament vision of the new world. This is the essence of black America's quest for the promised land.

The cathartic release generated by John's conversion serves to bind this isolated man-child to the members of the community. The full force of the epigraph from Revelation now comes into play:

> And the Spirit and the bride say, Come. And let him that heareth say, Come. And let him that is athirst come. And whosoever will, let him take the water of life freely. (22:17)

In the excerpt from Revelation, John, the man of Patmos, exhorts his fellow Christians, who like himself are oppressed and persecuted, to partake freely of "the water of life," which is another fulfillment of the reward offered by the martyr in Rev. 7:17 (Jesus).[32] This glorious invitation to say "yes" to God is the climax of the New Testament and of the Holy Scriptures. Unlike the three supplicants who failed to meet the qualification for salvation as expressed in his grandmother's prayer, John has the potential to realize his dreams.

Undoubtedly, a major contributing factor to the dynamic hold *Go Tell It on the Mountain* has on the reader's imagination is Baldwin's seamless integration of the cultural script of the black church idiom. Not only does he take the reader through the interiority of black life and culture, but also he explores the full implication of the

32. John of Patmos, or Saint John the Divine, was the author of the book of Revelation, or the Apocalypse. It was written on the penal island of Patmos in the Aegean Sea, where John had been banished, perhaps during the reign of Domitian, about A.D. 95. The island scene provided much imagery for John's visions of the New Jerusalem, the Lamb of God, the fall of Babylon, and Judgment Day.

route to psychic freedom that the sermon provides for a powerless black community. The sermon makes the reality of black people's lives bearable, enables them to retain their dignity, and orders the terror. Thus empowered, they are then able both to sing and to preach the Lord's song in a strange land. In this respect, Baldwin stands as a literary witness to black folk culture. He creatively engages the semantic transformation inherent in the sermon to make the transition from the communal vision of the folk imagination to the often private vision of the prose fiction writer.

On the one hand, Baldwin (like Douglass, Johnson, Hurston, Ellison, and Morrison) demonstrates his mastery of the general system of linguistic rules and regulations that govern the dominant society, while, on the other hand, he also demonstrates his fluency in black oral expressive literature. The sermon as well as the other black folk forms, though they may have developed, in many cases, from European or American models, was essentially of African derivation, subjected, of course, to the transformations that American life had brought into existence. The black folk sermon issues forth out of the ethos of the slave community, a community whose religious experience is colored by "the terror and frustration of day-to-day existence in a society in which the oppressor is identified as Christian."[33] Furthermore, the black sermon is a testament to black people's powers of conception, a suggestion that their ability to create, grasp, and use symbols is just as valid as those who oppress and would deny them their humanity. In other words, the black folk sermon as symbolic language must affirm something. This affirmation finds expression in John's apocalyptic vision:

> I, John, saw the future, way up in
>   the middle of the air.
> I, John, saw a number, way up in
>   the middle of the air.
> I, John, saw a city, way up in
>   the middle of the air,
> Waiting, waiting, waiting up there. (201, 204)

Translated by Baldwin into the symbolic language of his black sermon, John Grimes, like the man of Patmos, emerges steeled with

33. Jones, *Blues People,* 42, and Lincoln, *Black Church since Frazier,* 122.

the resolve expressed in the spiritual "Ain't Gonna Let Nobody Turn Me Around."[34]

From the standpoint of preacher and congregation, "go tell it on the mountain" and "let my people go" as mascons and as metaphors for black struggle connote redemption, liberation, and confederation. From the standpoint of writer and reader, "go tell it on the mountain" and "let my people go" are emblematic of Baldwin's liberating of the folk sermon from the normative demands of its cathartic function, while maintaining a fidelity to its vision of transformation, transcendence, and uplift. Like James Weldon Johnson in *God's Trombones,* Baldwin, at times with stunning grace, articulates the creative possibilities of the black church idiom as literary expression. Using the sermon as organizing principle, he transforms historical consciousness into art. He releases and reinforces the expressive power of black church idiom as interpretative language or hermeneutical tool as he figuratively steps out on space and time and dynamically recovers the voice and vision of the community as expressed in the preacher's encyclopedic observation, "I'll make me a world."

34. The Student Peace Union, comp., *Songs for Peace,* 42–43. See also James Baldwin, "The Death of the Prophet," 257–61. That Baldwin essentially agreed with Gabriel's skepticism following John's conversion is evident in "The Death of the Prophet," which may be read as a postscript to *Go Tell It on the Mountain.*

6

The Sermon and the Recovery of Community

Song of Solomon and *Beloved*

In her critically acclaimed *Song of Solomon* and *Beloved,* Toni Morrison explores and extends her meditation on history as she examines the debilitating effects of slavery and its aftermath on black America. *Beloved* begins where *Song of Solomon* ends: on the cusp between the Emancipation Proclamation and Reconstruction. In the first novel, she adheres more to the bildungsroman as she tells of the pursuit of manhood from the perspective of her thirty-two-year-old protagonist, whose father sacrifices his past for what he thinks is a secure future; in the second novel, she tells the tragic story of a recently escaped slave woman who kills her daughter rather than have her captured and returned to slavery. With a hagiography that includes Africans who can fly, a woman born without a navel, and ghosts, Morrison, in these "gothic fables," described by Bernard Bell as "poetic narratives whose celebration of the beauty, truth, and possibilities of life is derived from the exploitation of its magic, mystery, and terror,"[1] probes the interiority of black life as only as a skilled commentator can.

Song of Solomon and *Beloved* possess a virtuoso range of tones, and the good reader will learn to interpret them with a parallel virtuosity. Part of the success of these texts "is that [they] demand

1. *Afro-American Novel,* 270.

anticipated feedback in order to take place at all." Morrison anticipates our response, and her form and content are shaped accordingly. The method by which Morrison arranges those inconspicuous repetitions of word, idea, or incident—the literary devices that add up to what E. M. Forster called "rhythms"—may well owe something to the black sermonic tradition. At some points in *Song of Solomon* and *Beloved,* the harmonics of Morrison's tone are audible only when the listener is familiar with that background.[2]

Morrison plays off the sermon as an *ideology,* in contrast to the sermon as a *practice,* that emotionally arouses the people with words that are disconnected from the present reality. As ideology, Morrison's sermonic rhetoric is situated within the philosophical and aesthetic ideologies of Americans of African descent. I will examine Morrison's use of sermonic rhetoric with emphasis on the affirmation in *Song of Solomon* and the celebration in *Beloved* that instantiate a dialogic counterplay between the male and female voices of these texts. In *Beloved* Morrison appropriates a religious discourse that projects the self as male and black to show not only that the African American woman is defined in terms of her relation to her man but also that she can lift her voice to sing a song of the fallen woman.

Morrison presents the female voice as a corrective to the male biographical voice rooted in the black church. The female voice joins the male voice in a dialogue on the reconstruction and regeneration of community. Morrison makes the connection between sermonic discourse, self-determination, and spiritual authority as she engages in a progressive dialectic between memory (*Song of Solomon*) and forgetting (*Beloved*). For a different set of reasons, the journeys back of her male and female protagonists, which is ultimately about beginnings, about community, raise a number of questions—Can the pain in the community be healed? Can the redemptive vision be restored?—questions that recall the biblical text of Ezekiel's Old Testament query "Can these bones live?" (37:1–4).

Ezekiel was a priest who was deported to Babylonia at the capture of Jerusalem in 597 B.C. As a prophet to the exiles, he assured his hearers of the abiding presence of God among them. In ecstatic vision Ezekiel is transported to the valley ("plain" in 3:22 and 8:4)

2. Ong, *Orality and Literacy: The Technology of the Word,* 176; E. M. Forster, *Aspects of the Novel,* 213–47; and Kermode, "John," 454–55.

where earlier he had seen the glory of Jehovah and is made to pass up and down in it so that he may see how full it is of dry bones, which are the bleaching remnants of a slaughtered army and which are also the exiles themselves, who have no more hope of resuscitating the kingdom of Israel than of putting flesh on a skeleton and calling it to life. Jehovah bids him to prophesy to the bones; he will cause spirit to enter into them, they shall be clothed with human bodies, and they shall live. Morrison, it seems to me, acknowledges that Africans in America have been beaten and battered as a result of their enslavement, but they have not been defeated by it. She calls on the community to regroup (*Song of Solomon*) and draw strength from both the horror and the beauty of its legacy of enslavement (*Beloved*).[3]

And the Children May Know Their Names

In *Song of Solomon,* Morrison shifts the narrative focus from the tradition of uplift (with its accompanying exegesis on success or failure) to the anomalies of the American Dream. The Dead family becomes a trope for those blacks who migrated to the North and the Midwest in the wake of Reconstruction in order to escape from oppression. The marginalized Macon Dead severed the linkage with his sister born without a navel, closed the door on his southern roots, married the only daughter of the only black doctor in town, and became a somewhat successful businessman, albeit a borderline one. Macon makes an uneasy peace with his past, and, in his hasty retreat from agrarian culture, his embrace of industrial culture makes him hard and indifferent toward the needs of his family.

The journey toward the northern promised land generates a natural conceit, for truth itself becomes a kind of falsehood, a victim of the secular Eden. In his relentless drive for success as well as insulation from a hostile world, Macon Dead embalmed the legacy of his given name and buried many of the values associated with his past. Somewhere along the way, he forgot "that each individual is a precious secret essence; that society, and more particularly the industrial society, threatens these essences; that the old values of life

3. *Song of Solomon* (1987). All citations are from this edition and are hereafter noted by page numbers in parentheses.

have been destroyed by the industrial dispensation; that people have been cut off from each other and even from themselves."[4]

Macon sees Christianity as a sort of material salvation for himself and his family; he defines happiness as "owning things" (163, 234, 300), which goes against the grain of the corporate imagination. Morrison suggests that Macon's relentless push for success and economic independence signifies a blind faith that borders on unquestioning idolatry, as is evident from his keeping the two keys in his pocket juxtaposed to Pilate's wearing her name in a brass box earring. The two keys are emblematic of Macon's stake in the American Dream. Symbolically, Pilate wearing her name in a brass box earring suggests that she has not rejected her history. We should not lose sight of the fact that Macon's objective is to make his children replicas of others in their socioeconomic class; he turns them into social showpieces, especially his daughters.

The transformation in his son known as Milkman occurs when he is shocked into seeing his family history in a new light in Danville, Pennsylvania. Milkman's odyssey is as much a search for gold as it is a search for self. Work, authority, and decision making are symbolized by Macon Dead, and Milkman's longing for flight is defined against him. Whereas Invisible Man strives for the American Dream and fails, Macon Dead achieves it to some extent but, since he does not face his history, his achievement is bereft of joy. The white power brokers greet his hard-won success with indifference. The impoverished blacks greet it with a mixture of silent anger and grudging admiration. Macon suffers a fate common to an emergent bourgeoisie: he is suspended between two worlds and belongs to neither. He overcompensates for his class insecurity by using his money to shield his children from their history. Consequently, they have little social contact with their reference community. Is it any wonder that Macon Dead's family is in disarray?

When compared to the world of the "classic" black preacher (as represented by preachers such as John Jasper), Macon Dead represents the *crack* in the archaic imagination, though he himself was shaped by the idiom and character of the historic black church; now in the industrial Babylon with its diminished promise, he stands as the end product of the loss of faith or, more precisely, the failure of

4. Lionel Trilling, *The Liberal Imagination,* 27.

religion to sanction his single-minded vision, as is evident when Lena releases the full fury of her pent-up anger on Milkman because of his self-centered world. Essentially a kept man and insensitive to the feelings of his sisters, Milkman, as a matter of privilege, decides who is not an appropriate suitor for his sister Corinthians (215–17).

As part of her narrative strategy, Morrison uses sermonic rhetoric to assay how Macon's quest for freedom becomes a falsehood, which turns him into a grotesque, and to liberate his son from the text, from the values of an industrial culture that has become abstract without life. Morrison uses sermonic rhetoric both to draw our attention to the anomalies of the American Dream and to point the way toward the recovery of community. Her silent texts are the return of the Prodigal Son and Lazarus rising from the grave. These texts that revoice Luke's parables about the lost (15:4–32) illustrate Morrison's concern for a community that has lost contact with its history. Morrison uses the Prodigal Son parable to illustrate the high cost of assimilation for black America. Prodded by his Aunt Pilate, Milkman wakes up from a life buried under materialism. He will come to rejoice and call on his community to share in his joy. The economy of slavery has deadened the community to its contribution to American culture. In his journey back, Milkman undergoes a Lazarus-like transformation, which is the cause for his rejoicing: *my (our) history was dead, and is alive; it was lost, and is found.*[5] Morrison's moral is, clearly, that if African Americans bury their history, material wealth alone will not convince them they have arrived in the promised land.

The songs that enrich the narrative landscape stand as dynamic counterpoint to the biblical narratives of prodigality. For example, Pilate's singing is an exegesis on compassion and tenderness extended to all regardless of their station in life. This exegesis—which reaches its climax at Hagar's funeral—is all the more ironic because her medium of expression is the blues and not the Christian church. Yet her message is one with which all Christians can identify: the recovery of community begins with the recovery of the self and the ability to place oneself in the place of another.

5. Luke 15:11–32 is a series of parables about the lost: the lost sheep, the lost coin, and the lost son. Luke 16:19–31 tells the story of the rich man and Lazarus, and John 11:1–57 tells of the raising of Lazarus. Combining the two narratives, Morrison investigates what it means to be an African American.

Morrison directs attention to chapter 10, the philosophical center of the narrative, by invoking sermonic rhetoric to indicate a change in the orientation of her protagonist as he moves from strident individualism toward recognition of group ethos. As narrative strategy, Morrison's use of sermonic rhetoric enables her to shift her focus from I-It to I-Thou relationships. This does not mean that Milkman becomes more saintly; instead, he only becomes less self-centered, as is evident during the ritual hunt in the woods in Virginia when he reflects on his indifferent attitude toward his family and his one-sided relationship with his first cousin–lover, Hagar (300–301).

Milkman's odyssey gains its intensity from his realization that his ancestors invested land with a religious significance. When hope gave place to expectation, black people, who had been enslaved for close to 250 years, were not merely content with freedom when it came. They wanted land as a sign of their social inclusion in the body politic, as is evident in the expression "forty acres and a mule." Driven by corporate desire that crested in the years immediately following the Emancipation Proclamation, the African American imagination's idea of land became a sacred thing rather than merely a social address from the backwoods of Georgia to the outskirts of the nameless midwestern town Macon Dead calls home. This, in part, explains the defeated hope written on the faces of Milkman's father's childhood friends who gather at the home of Rev. Cooper.[6] They looked to Milkman's grandfather, Macon Dead, Sr., for their inspiration.

From the perspective of his father's childhood friends, his grandfather had emerged from the numberless valleys "of the shadow of death" with the vigor and vitality necessary to wrest a livelihood from a forbidding land. The lush Pennsylvania forest, with its tall hardwoods and stone jutting out like the ribs of prehistoric creatures and its crisp, clear, sparkling night, were in no sense alien to him. Instead, they were the signposts of his home in Montour County, Pennsylvania. His farm was a testament to his abiding faith in the infinite possibility of life in America, and it confirmed the preacher's unending declaration that "there is a God somewhere!"

6. The religious connotations associated with land in the black American context are evident in the rich body of song and folklore. See Jones, *Blues People;* Lovell, *Black Song;* Harding, *There Is a River;* and Dena J. Epstein, *Sinful Tunes and Spirituals: Black Folk Music to the Civil War.*

The green pastures and still waters of his picturesque farm called upon his fellow freedmen to *look, behold, hearken, wait, watch, lift up their eyes.* It seems that he was ever unaware either of danger or of the envy that lurked in the eyes of his white neighbors. Because of his success in spite of his proximity to danger, his life spoke to his fellow weary travelers in a strange land of his heroism, his initiative, his powers of endurance, his contribution to the common good—in short, his *value.*

It is this value that the preacher holds in high esteem and celebrates from his pulpit, for it embodies the heroic soul of a long-suffering people. Thus, in spite of their oppression, they, like the "fabulous Macon Dead," developed an "ideal of justice to kinsman and stranger"[7] that found its expression in their oral tradition. And to Milkman's grandfather, that amazing fount of never-failing life owed its source in large part to those anonymous black preachers who, stealing away under the cover of darkness to the praise house or marching up and down their pulpits, challenged their brothers and sisters to step out on space and time and make themselves a world.

There is, then, far more than meets the eye of the cursory reader in the repetitive "never mind" (and similar phrases) that sprinkle Morrison's description of the land. By repeating the same words, she recovers black people's accomplishment in the short period of Reconstruction as they strove mightily to make America home. The phrase *never mind* is, then, a synecdoche that, in suggesting the heroic drive of the corporate imagination, carries theological weight that invests *land* and *home* with intense spiritual energy. Morrison concisely characterizes the "fabulous Macon Dead" (236) (and his childhood friends, the men with "rheumy eyes" [234], of whom he is the eponymous father) with the thumbnail portrait of his self-centered, underachieving grandson. She collapses the dialectic of

7. Mary Ellen Chase, *Life and Language in the Old Testament,* 23–26. It seems to me that in her description of Macon Dead's farm, Morrison tries to recover the sense of innocence, wonder, and excitement that many of the newly freed former slaves must have felt in the wake of Emancipation. The years of suffering that black people had endured enabled them to own the land in a way that their oppressors did not. It is in this sense that her recovery of this moment shares an affinity with the writers of the Old Testament, "who," as Chase observes, "are constantly calling upon their readers or hearers to *look, behold, hearken, wait, watch, listen, lift up their eyes*" (25).

correspondence and difference between grandfather and grandson once Milkman begins to respond to the multiple levels of meaning embedded in *land* and *home.*

As a representative of the corporate imagination in its search for wholeness, Milkman arrives in a western Pennsylvania town that time forgot in search of gold to enrich his material life; instead, he discovers his rich heritage and departs for Virginia with the skeletal details that can connect him to his family tree. Beginning with his aunt, Pilate, who makes him aware of the levels of meaning attached to his name, and picking up momentum in Danville with the old men and Circe, who engender in him a "desire" to know more about his history, Milkman begins the process of turning the outer world (that is, received cultural and social opinion) into an inner speech as he (re)connects himself with the voice and vision of his aesthetic community, which culminates in the forest of Virginia. He thus gains an appreciation for his culture as well as a grounding in the soil that produced the blues, spirituals, and folklore. He now understands the rhythms that govern the life of his father, Aunt Pilate, and Guitar. In short, Milkman discovers a face that, heretofore, he had not been able to see: his own.

Upon Milkman's return from the grave, as it were, the astonished men at Rev. Cooper's echo the words of Luke, "Let us eat, and make merry; for this my son was dead, and is alive again" (15:23–24 Revised Standard Version). Having lost contact with his father, Macon Dead, their childhood playmate, they had considered him for all intents and purposes "dead" in that far country. While Macon's childhood friends freely accept the return of the grandson of the "fabulous Macon Dead," Macon unbeknownst to them prospered in that far country. As the long gone prodigal son, Macon Dead, unrepentant, prospered under circumstances that tried his soul. He now is in a position to exclaim, "This is the life!" This is the meaning of his ritual Sunday drives with his family; they are meaningful not so much for what they say to his family as for what they say to the world. Macon Dead represents that historic moment when blacks break with their agrarian background, identify with bourgeois values, yet lack a language in which to define themselves.[8]

8. In the middle section of *Cane,* Jean Toomer anticipates black people breaking with their agrarian background. "Rhobert" is his signature piece on black people's

However, unlike the long lost son in the parable, black people's place in American society is not freely restored. The psychic toll is incalculable. Out of the resulting existential despair emerge the blues.

From this perspective, Macon Dead's life represents the liminal antithesis of the aspirations of his childhood friends. Their dream associates the restorative properties of land with freedom, rejuvenation, and dignity. Macon associates land with possession, ownership, and commodity (as, incidentally, he sees his daughters). The price Macon pays for his freedom—this is the hidden cost that the men do not see, and Milkman wisely does not attempt to explain the loss of soul. Milkman will work gradually to free himself from a text that signifies a rejection of community. We read Milkman's coming to Danville as a "sign" that points to a fulfillment, not only in the men's remembrance of things past but also in Milkman's growing awareness of the linkage between historical consciousness and present actions. Danville signifies the loss of temporal place that is necessary for Milkman to recover his spiritual place.

For Milkman, an hour has come, a choice has been made, and the hour and the choice are themselves of a decisive importance. The visit with the men at Rev. Cooper's, at a deeper level, negates his father's representational truths in order to symbolize the undecidability that undermines all acts of understanding.[9] Correspondingly, as Milkman grows into consciousness, he grows beyond the secular hell of his spiritual emptiness.

Milkman's inward turn to the self begins when Rev. Cooper says, "I know your people!" (229), which is to say that he knows his history, both its luminous beauty and its terrible horror. Rev. Cooper pulls Milkman away from his individual ethic and toward the community—the people—that he as figurative prodigal son has abandoned. Milkman gains his history, as it were, through the blending of voices in this homecoming scene as he listens to the old men

---

complicity in their own destruction in the urban metropolis. Others who treat this crack in the corporate imagination include writers such as Dunbar, *Sport of the Gods;* Wallace Thurman, *Harlem;* and Langston Hughes, *Not without Laughter.*

9. Ramon Saldivar, *Figural Language in the Novel: The Flowers of Speech from Cervantes to Joyce,* 23–24. See also Karla F. C. Holloway, "*Beloved:* A Spiritual." Of central interest to Holloway in *Beloved* is how "narrative structures have been consciously manipulated through a complicated interplay between the implicit orature of recovered and (re)membered events and the explicit structures of literature" (516).

who visit him at Rev. Cooper's house reconstruct and reconnect him to his past. They authenticate the stories his father has told him: "These men remembered both Macon Deads as extraordinary men. . . . The more the old men talked—the more he heard about the only farm in the county that grew peaches, real peaches like they had in Georgia, the feasts they had when hunting was over, the pork kills in the winter and the work, the backbreaking work of a going farm—the more he missed something in his life" (234). The old men thus provide Milkman with a grammar for understanding the heretofore inexplicable emptiness that gnaws away at Guitar's and his life. The story the men tell "of the fabulous Macon Dead" (236), the liminality of it, is now deepened into myth, and the myth is dressed in representation of actuality.[10] Morrison situates human awareness in continuity. Milkman is the word made flesh.

Milkman discovers that the power of words and words of power, like *freedom,* acquire a life of their own, over and apart from the day-to-day oppression that the people may experience: "His own father's words came back to him: 'I worked right alongside my father. Right alongside him.' Milkman thought then that his father was boasting of his manliness as a child. Now he knew he had been saying something else. That he loved his father; had an intimate relationship with him . . . and found him worthy of working 'right alongside him'" (234). In telling Milkman his history, Macon, like the preacher (and these old men), ritualizes the experience as he sings the song of the fallen man. Caught up in the emotional moment in Rev. Cooper's living room, Milkman realizes that for the first time he truly hears the meaning behind the words his father told of the love for his father. In this recognition scene, Milkman discovers that Macon, his "stern, greedy, unloving [father]" (234), had provided him with information to articulate the self in a hostile world.

Inherent in the sermon as a modality of black expression is its coming to grips with cultural disruption and transformation. This is the unsaid that fuels the dynamic exchange between Milkman and the old men who visit him at Rev. Cooper's. Whereas he sees defeated hope written in their eyes, they see his father, and particularly his grandfather, as the sermon they were not allowed to

10. Kermode, "John," 448.

become: "Macon Dead was the farmer they wanted to be, the clever irrigator, the peach-tree grower, the hog slaughterer, the wild-turkey roaster, the man who could plow forty in no time flat and sang like an angel while he did it" (235). Thus the old men's ritualization of communal pain in song and story overrides, if momentarily, the difference between their daily experience and their faith that one of them will break through the wall of oppression. It is in this sense that we can say that Macon is the sermon they were not allowed to become. And Milkman, "the [grand]son of the fabulous Macon Dead" (236), is the sermon yet to be preached.

The ritual power of the sermon, as is evident in the previously mentioned passage, is made manifest in Morrison's consecration of the land in one of the most moving passages in contemporary black American literature. Reminiscent of James Weldon Johnson's preacher-as-creator in "The Creation," Morrison captures the sense of metaphorical possibility I have in mind when the preacher-as-creator says, "I'll make me a world." Stepping out on space and time, she imaginatively re-creates the infinite promise and possibility freedom held for the newly freed slaves. Through their actions, they made the word flesh, the word being *freedom,* as they arrived in their promised land, symbolized by the patriarchal Macon Dead, who named his farm Lincoln's Heaven. After sixteen years of backbreaking work, his farm "colored their lives like a paintbrush and spoke to them like a sermon":

> "You see?" the farm said to them. "See? See what you can do? Never mind you can't tell one letter from another, never mind you born a slave, never mind you lose your name, never mind your daddy dead, never mind nothing. Here, this here, is what a man can do if he puts his mind to it and his back in it. Stop sniveling," it said. "Stop picking around the edges of the world. Take advantage, and if you can't take advantage, take disadvantage. We live here. On this planet, in this nation, in this country right here. *No*where else! We got a home in the rock, don't you see! Nobody starving in my home, nobody crying in my home, and if I got a home you got one too!" (235)

In this passage, Morrison replicates sermonic structure with the ritualized repetition of "never mind." She reminds us of the oral tradition that undergirds performance in the black community. Moreover, Morrison invokes the black preacher's use of emotionally powerful image clusters—mascons. For example, the mascon-filled phrase "We got a home in the rock" is a cultural clue for the community blacks erected to ward off the hostility of a discriminating white America.[11] Behind the surge and roll of this lyrical language, Morrison is talking about how the word *community* once sustained black people. In the industrial Babylon, it has been emptied of much of its meaning.

Like the preacher, Morrison's narrator makes the words express that which is in the hearts of these old men with "pitiful hungry eyes" (250). Using "verbal arpeggios, the cascading adjectives, and the rhythmic repetitions," Morrison's narrator-preacher takes the woolly-haired Jesus from the lofty throne of a faraway heaven and makes Him a part of the people's daily rituals—rituals of toil, despair, triumph.[12] They see, hear, and touch Him as He walks a mile in their shoes, as is evident in the concluding flourish to Macon Dead's sermon: "Grab this land! Take it, hold it, my brothers, make it, my brothers, shake it, squeeze it, turn it, twist it, beat it, kick it, kiss it, whip it, stomp it, dig it, plow it, seed it, reap it, rent it, sell it, own it, build it, multiply it, and pass it on—can you hear me? Pass it on!" (235)

Like thousands of newly freed slaves, the Deads, too, were caught up in post–Civil War euphoria; hope and dreams were ascendant. Freedom held for them the distinct possibility that they would assume a meaningful place in the nation's official history. The dramatic tension in the recognition scene stems from Milkman's realization of the cruel trick history had played on the black community, smashing their expectations. In one fell swoop paradise was both gained and lost. He sees his grandfather's bloody end as a metaphor for black life in America.

Morrison's point in this elegiac account of lost tomorrows is not that Milkman emerges Christlike from the figurative laying on of hands by the old men as they reconstruct his history; her use of sermonic rhetoric signals the enlargement of his self-centered vision. Having become "born again" by the dramatic retelling of his family history, Milkman desires the gold, as material gain and as cultural legacy. The gold symbolizes the answer to the spiritual

11. Henderson, *Understanding the New Black Poetry*, 43–45.
12. Barksdale, "Margaret Walker," 105.

emptiness—the absence of a legacy—that gnaws away at Guitar's and his insides. Milkman wants to "run to where it was and snatch every grain of it from under the noses of the Butlers, who were dumb enough to believe that if they killed one man his whole line died" (236).

Milkman's journey back may be seen as a moving parable of the spirit. His message to Pilate on the discovery of his golden heritage (and, hence, the first stirring of community) is tantamount to the good news like Ezekiel's sermons calling Judah to repentance, which would be apostrophes spoken in Babylonia. Morrison reverses the good news with Milkman's message from the "old country" to those who are living a buried life in exile in the hope that report of them would reach the intended audience. We should note that Morrison is careful not to romanticize Milkman's return to what Baldwin refers to in the title essay from his *Nobody Knows My Name* as "the old country, [a place] which he has never seen, but which [he] cannot fail to recognize" (86). Milkman comes to terms with his repressed and unrealized desire to be a man—responsible, productive, intimate. Prior to this threshold moment, Milkman wanted freedom but without risk.[13]

When the full meaning of his buried history flowers in his imagination as a result of his decoding a supposedly innocuous rhyme sung by the children of Shalimar, Milkman's perception of reality is altered forever (300–303). He no longer views his name (as metaphor for the collective buried history of his community) as a tomb.[14] His world is born anew, for he walks with a new walk and talks a new talk, as is evident in his euphoric bus ride home to share the "good news" with Pilate:

> How many dead lives and fading memories were buried in and beneath the names of the places in this country. Under the recorded names were other names, just as 'Macon Dead,' recorded for all time in some dusty file, hid from view the real names of people, places, and things. Names that had meaning. No wonder

13. "Nobody Knows My Name: A Letter from the South," in Baldwin, *Nobody Knows My Name*, 86. Also see Terry Otten, *The Crime of Innocence in the Fiction of Toni Morrison*, 51.

14. Douglass, *Narrative*, 105. A recurring motif in the writings of Douglass is his description of slavery as a "tomb," an institution that literally and figuratively kills the spirit.

> Pilate put hers in her ear. When you know your name, you should hang on to it, for unless it is noted down and remembered, it will die when you do. (329)

He discovers that blacks have had the power of *naming* stolen from them. They have not been free to use their power to name themselves, the world, or God. Words are power; language is power; he has the capacity to free himself from the image that other people have of him. The names become a symbolic space where Milkman can imagine freedom. And the power, majesty, and triumph of history, of naming, flashes before him in the children's rhyme. So overwrought is he by this discovery that he becomes intoxicated not with happiness but with joy (as the old preacher would put it). As he becomes more enmeshed in names and naming, Milkman undergoes ritual transformation as well. The history that Milkman discovers behind the buried names transforms his journey back into a mission fraught with religious overtones; hence his insatiable need to proclaim.

Power in the ability to name as well as recognition of the effort is what causes the people to pay "their respect to whatever it was that made [Milkman's maternal grandfather] *be* a doctor in the first place, when the odds were that he'd be a yardman all of his life" (329). The underlying reality is that these ordinary people brought a certain intelligence to the task before them and created a culture. Ultimately, what transforms Milkman from his narrow self-centeredness is his recognition that he bears witness to a great tradition (330).

The misnaming of the Deads is a metaphoric dramatization of Morrison's thesis that *forms and patterns* are more pervasive and persistent in their influence on society than what they contain. A fundamental pattern of the discourse of racism is the disruption of black families as a result of black people's radical otherness in America and their entrapment in a form of neo-slavery.[15]

To deprive a community of its name is to devalue its worth and deprive it of its place in a dynamic history. It represents the separation and distortion of the personality. At bottom, to deprive a com-

15. Carby, "Ideologies of Black Folk," 125–43. I borrow the term *neo-slavery* from Carby's discussion of the folk in black fiction, which limits discussion of the black middle class.

munity of the ability to name itself is a theologically based form of oppression that traps and enslaves. If the first act that follows creation in Genesis is naming, then deprivation of this right subverts the theological legacy and disenfranchises the owners of the word. If you cannot *name,* you cannot call the world into order. Of what use is the dynamism of the word? To not own your name is tantamount to not owning your history. It is a sign of the broken covenant between God and humanity schematized as racism. Hence the cultural imperative that the preacher sing the song of a fallen community. Morrison appropriates this language of religion and integrates it into the structure of her narrative.

Having reclaimed his buried history, Milkman—unlike his great-grandfather Jake (or Shalimar, as he was known in these parts), whose inability to name, to call the world into order, prompted his flying back to Africa—stands on the precipice of calling the world into order. In the process, Milkman fulfills the prophecy "And the children shall know their names." Morrison thus makes it clear that the black American story must be rescued from a buried history; and she fervently understands her own endeavor as literary witness.

Morrison holds out the possibility that "these bones [can] live"; the recovery of community continues to unfold for Americans of African descent in the United States. Yet Milkman, her protagonist, is not able to reintegrate himself into the community, as is evident by the problematic ending of the novel. How do we explain this denial of closure? How do we explain this rupture in the romantic tradition, of which the sermon is an essential component in this utopian ideology? Morrison disrupts the salvational and wish-fulfilling utopian conclusion of romance in order to emphasize that as long as Milkman's humanity is called into question (and by implication that of the community), he will not be accepted by the body politic in good standing. Until this acceptance happens, the community will not be able to right itself and get about the business of healing and reconciliation.

A Story to Pass On

As mentioned above, *Beloved* begins where *Song of Solomon* ends—amidst the struggles of the Reconstruction years. Morrison has remembered the nineteenth-century reality of a slave woman named

Margaret Garner into a universe of "sixty million and more" dry bones who are "of this story." Set in the outskirts of Cincinnati in 1873, *Beloved,* through a series of flashbacks with a sympathetic omniscient narrator, tells the tragic story of Sethe Suggs, who escaped from slavery in Kentucky but is haunted by profound guilt over the killing of her daughter, whose ghost traumatizes the family. Once the focal point of much of the social activity in the black community, the house at 124 Bluestone Road is now noted for its isolation as a result of Sethe's act of "criminal love."[16] Her act represents the crisis of consciousness in a world turned upside down; the enormity of the horror is the brutal response to a mode of production that systematically engaged in the quintessential separation—that of mother from child. Sethe's desperate ferocity shocked all beholders.

Tormented by her incipient guilt and the return of the demonic Beloved, Sethe, isolated from the day-to-day discourse of the community, responds with a defiant arrogance as she locks herself away from the people who can help her to lay her burden down. When it appears that Beloved's ghost will suck all of the life out of her mother in its vengeful quest, Denver, nearing her twentieth birthday, reaches out to the community of women, who band together to drive evil from their midst. The spiritual strength the women find deep within themselves lends a note of triumph and celebration to their endeavor.

Sethe's unpardonable act devastates and nearly shocks into silence her mother-in-law, Baby Suggs, who has spent the majority of "her sixty years a slave and ten years free" counseling blacks not to surrender to despair.[17] Nothing in Baby Suggs's system of values condones the abnormal behavior of her daughter-in-law; an immoral system does not absolve one of moral responsibility. Her theology of history, formed in the crucible of slavery, is shattered. Shortly after Sethe's attempt to slay her family, injuring her two sons and killing Beloved, Baby Suggs, charismatic preacher, gives up on life and seeks peace in colors. Brokenhearted, Baby Suggs soon dies.

In ideological terms, Baby Suggs as cultural worker represents

16. Otten, *Crime of Innocence,* 82.

17. *Beloved* (1987), 104. All citations are from this edition and are hereafter noted by page numbers in parentheses.

the spontaneous bias in a social system that does not, indeed cannot, meet the needs of a structurally silent people in general and of black women in particular. Morrison presents Baby Suggs as a preacher in exile in response to those black men who perpetuate against black women the exclusive practices they condemn in white men by establishing their experience as normative in the black community, which recalls Ezekiel's Old Testament query "Can these bones live?" Black men endow their representation of self with the weight of spiritual aspiration and universal truth. Morrison not only appropriates this male-centered discourse, but she also executes a subtle but perceptive role reversal. Baby Suggs can as easily be brought into the blues tradition (confrontational) as Sethe can be brought into the spiritual tradition (transcendence). Baby Suggs's sermon, which stands at the moral center of this Gothic fable, is a reminder of the shifting field of interpretation that takes place.[18]

Baby Suggs's spatial position is emblematic of her emotional isolation from the organized church. She undermines the image of God as male as well as the myth of the church as sanctuary for women. Sethe's isolation, therefore, cannot be understood apart from Baby Suggs's isolation from the church. And finally, Baby Suggs's distance from the organized church prefigures her granddaughter seeking an-other route to salvation within the community of women.

Baby Suggs, modeled on women drawn to the life of itinerant evangelism, such as Sojourner Truth and Jarena Lee, stands as Morrison's tribute to those stellar figures who midwifed the black community along the pathway from slavery to freedom. Like many of her unsung sisters, Baby Suggs possesses a physical as well as a "spiritual heroism."[19] She epitomizes those individuals who held the fragmented community together in the face of adversity. She depends on personal experience and charisma rather than training as the basis for her ministry. In the "Esther" section of Toomer's *Cane,* the sexually potent Barlo depends on his personal experience and charisma as well as his vitality. Much of Baby Suggs's appeal stems from her authentic, direct religion as well as from her grounding in a rich humanistic tradition.

18. Trudier Harris, "From Exile to Asylum: Religion and Community in the Writings of Contemporary Black Women," 151–69.

19. Andrews, *Sisters of the Spirit,* 2.

In her hour of greatest need, Baby Suggs, confronted with a "choice between Christian resignation or faith and humanistic action or reason,"[20] opts for the latter code of ethics. The Christian God does not provide answers for the enormity of the horror she has witnessed, nor does He explain the unrelenting terror of the white community. For one who is considered "holy" (89) and is compelled to preach, her Sunday sermons in the Clearing now take on a much harsher edge in the wake of the unimaginable tragedy that befalls her family. She draws the attention of the new arrivals to Cincinnati to the things of this world, not the things in the world to come. Baby Suggs does not preach a gospel of personal conversion as the answer to all problems, which shares an affinity with Pilate's blues.

As an "unchurched preacher" (87) Baby Suggs does not offer up the gospel of the organized church but rather celebrates the freedom to be "in this here place, we flesh; flesh that weeps, laughs; flesh that dances on bare feet in grass. Love it. Love it hard. Yonder they do not love your flesh. They despise it" (88).

Referring to the destructive white culture "yonder," Baby Suggs tells the blacks gathered at the Clearing that "the only grace" they can have is "the grace they [can] imagine." Rejecting allegiance to a church too often hostage to the power that denied her all her eight children except Halle and crippled her body, she instructs the gathering to love the "flesh" that "here" abides in freedom, and "more than your life-holding wombs and your life-giving private parts, hear me now, love your heart. For this is the prize" (88–89). In spite of her "great heart," her faith in the recuperative powers of her people, and her insistence on self-love, Baby Suggs, as Otten observes, "cannot counter the enormity of evil (and love) that destroys Beloved."[21] This charismatic figure can find no words to erase the unspeakable horror and her complicity in the death of her granddaughter. She blames the whites: "The heart that pumped out love, the mouth that spoke the Word, didn't count. They came in her yard anyway and she could not oppose or condemn Sethe's rough choice" (180). Wise beyond her years, Denver sees through her grandmother's bedridden state. Baby Suggs knows "the ghost [is]

20. Trudier Harris, "Three Black Women Writers and Humanism: A Folk Perspective," 52.

21. Otten, *Crime of Innocence*, 88.

after Ma'am and her too for not doing anything to stop it [the murder]" (209).

Baby Suggs's advice to the embittered and guilt-ridden Sethe, "Lay em down, Sethe, Sword and shield. . . . Don't study war no more. Lay all that mess down" (86), is the leitmotif of the narrative. She reminds Sethe of the futility of running away from grief and of the destructive nature of guilt. Baby Suggs knows that one cannot run away from one's grief; she must confront it or forever be held hostage to it. Having been allowed to keep one of her eight children, this heavy-hearted mother reminds Sethe that all in the community can testify to the scattered bones of their loved ones: "Not a house in the country ain't packed to its rafters with some dead Negro's grief" (5). The letting go of the grief forms the centerpiece of the Sunday sermons Baby Suggs preaches to the new arrivals to Cincinnati as she fervently challenges them to "lay all that mess down," to lay down their loss, hurt, anger, and rejection in the land of their birth and go about the business of putting their lives back together.

The Clearing has symbolic reference in its name—a space to "clear" away grief. It serves multiple functions. First, it is a place where the fragmented community can beat back memories and broker the communal pain because an individual should not have to bear his or her pain alone. Second, it is a place where members of the fragmented community can imagine freedom, where the recovery of self and voice can begin as individuals make the emotional transference from seeing self as object to seeing self as subject. Third, as a precursor to the storefront church, the Clearing serves as a transition for the newcomers as they move from the perceived backwardness of folk religion to the respectability of the institutional black church, represented by the teacher, Lady Jones (247). And lastly, the Clearing as temple is a place where the community can begin to enforce its acceptable forms of behavior, clarify its social relationships, and revitalize its sense of responsibility to past, present, and future. Baby Suggs's sermon brings into visibility preacher and community as her words spoken "from the heart" and heard "in the heart" identify their weaknesses and strengths. With the people's mind attuned properly and their consciousness raised sufficiently, they are more than receptive to her charge that they "lay all that mess down" (86) and get on with their lives.

Behind Baby Suggs's reference to sword and shield lies the idea, so constant in Jewish eschatology, that the powers of good should finally vanquish the powers of evil. Prior to Sethe's unimaginable sin, Baby Suggs resolutely put on God's armor to fight, in the words of Paul, "principalities . . . hosts of wickedness" (Eph. 6:10–20). The forces of malevolent spirit beings are members of the slaveocracy, and its sympathizers organized to suppress the humanity of black people. If Baby Suggs is speaking of that perpetual struggle with evil that in its various phases always lies before the Christian, how can she effectively preach out against it with evil in her own home? (She is associated with that evil, and therefore she cannot preach effectively; this contributes to her resignation.) Sethe's action violates the fundamental moral principles by which Baby Suggs lives her life. By her ungodly action, Sethe displaces the moral high ground.

On her deathbed, the bereaved Baby Suggs asserts with conviction "that there was no bad luck in the world but white people. 'They don't know when to stop'" (104). Following the tragic events at 124 Bluestone, Baby Suggs had concluded that she had lied to her following and accordingly had revised her assessment of grace: "There was no grace—imaginary or real—and no sunlit dance in a Clearing could change that. Her faith, her love, her imagination and her great big old heart began to collapse twenty-eight days after her daughter-in-law arrived" (89). What finally crushes Baby Suggs's spirit is the emotional isolation the family is placed under. This is unbearable for one whose life personifies service and dedication to community. She exemplifies the artist as a witness or testifier. Staring into the abyss of her daughter-in-law's heart of darkness, Baby Suggs can no longer do either with certainty.

Nine years after the death of Baby Suggs, feeling the weight of her family's emotional isolation, Sethe returns to the Clearing with Beloved and Denver because she associates it with a happier, more tranquil time ("it was still the green blessed place she remembered" [89]), an Edenic moment in contrast to the false Eden of the plantation ironically named Sweet Home. It is the site of much of the happiness she shared with the community during the twenty-eight days of "unslaved life" she had known (95). She wants at "least to listen to the spaces that the long-ago singing had left behind" (89). She also returns to pay tribute to Halle.

Most of all, Sethe returns to the Clearing in search of how to lay her burden down and come to terms with her guilt. Will Beloved forgive her killing mother love? Will Sethe be able to imagine grace? The answer to the first question is not long in coming as the demonic Beloved tries to kill Sethe in this sacred space. The answer to the second question begins to unfold gradually once Denver confronts the ephemeral spirit after it attempts to choke Sethe. Over the next several months, Denver watches as the ghost of her dead sister nearly sucks the life out of her mother. To put an end to the vengeance, Denver reaches out to the community of women, many of whom as girls had played in her grandmother's yard. As David Smith notes, "Only when Sethe's ties to the community are reestablished does her salvation become possible" (197).[22] Denver is the bridge that reconnects her mother to the community and provides the impetus for a redefinition of grace and salvation.

What is implicit in Baby Suggs's standing outside the traditional church becomes explicit at the novel's conclusion. Salvation for black women lies within the restructuring of the process of salvation. Women have the power within themselves to commune with the divine and thereby save themselves, as Paul D observes to a reinvigorated Sethe: "You your best thing, Sethe. You are" (273). The success of the lay circle of women in driving out the evil spirit is a sign not of personal ability but of divine presence.[23] In the process, they validate the vision of Baby Suggs and snatch victory from the jaws of defeat. Sethe has come full circle as she has returned from exile to community.

In the context of a black American narrative code, Morrison recovers the sermon as a repressed black American formalism. She reconfigures this narrative code in order to disrupt the textual rhythm of the Gothic novel. For example, "Lay down your burden" functions in much the same way as does "a thematic marker throughout a sermon," in the words of Walter Pitts. It is stressed with a degree of regularity in the text in anticipation of the celebratory climax. Morrison subtly connects this thematic marker to the autobiographical voice and the creation of what Gates refers to as an "integral,

22. David Smith, "'Not to Need Permission for Desire—Well Now, That *Was* Freedom,'" 197.

23. Maya Deren, *Divine Horsemen: The Living Gods of Haiti,* 249. See also Walter Pitts, "West African Poetics in the Black Preaching Style," 146.

black self" as she recovers the voice of the preacher when the women come together to drive evil from their midst.[24]

The community of women who gather at 124 Bluestone Road share the same sentiments as do the women in Ntozake Shange's *For Colored Girls Who Have Considered Suicide When the Rainbow Is Enuf:* "i found god in myself & i loved her."[25] These women's reliance on each other is born of the experiential relationship that exists between black men and women as a result of the slave experience and the ensuing vestiges of slavery. The community, which reclaims the collective power of the word by articulating its voice as a chorus, is itself in need of resurrection.

Morrison enters a process of interpretation in which the church and extrachurch forms bring out the "synchrony" of the people's experience with events stored in the cultural memory. She is so adept that she is able to transcend the symmetry that the novel more or less imposes on her. When she overlays Baby Suggs's sermon, Paul D's blues, and the celebratory conclusion, the effect is actually greater than the sum of the three individual scenes. They comment on and support Sethe's transformation to a spiritual figure.

To ask "Can these bones live?" is to engage the dialectical unfolding of the phases through which memory and forgetting pass as black Americans try to deal with their enslavement as an integral part of their history. To ask "Can these bones live?" is really to assert the sovereignty of the African American story within American discourse. Morrison uses sermonic constructs not only as a shorthand to signal her congruence with this project but also to mine the "fictive" elements of the sermon as black American cultural production.

24. Pitts, "West African Poetics," 142. See also Henry Louis Gates, Jr., *Figures in Black: Words, Signs, and the "Racial" Self,* 115.

25. *For Colored Girls Who Have Considered Suicide When the Rainbow Is Enuf,* 63.

7

Voices and Visions

The triumph of the sermon in the black American literary imagination is a triumph of aesthetics. The sermon and the other black folk forms, though they may have developed, in many cases, from European or American models, were essentially of African derivation, subjected of course to the transformations that American life had brought about. The black folk sermon issued forth out of the ethos of the slave community, a community whose religious experience was colored by "the terror and frustration of day-to-day existence in a society in which the oppressor is identified as Christian."[1]

Furthermore, the black sermon is a testament to black people's powers of conception, a suggestion that their abilities to create, grasp, and use symbols are just as valid as those who oppress and would deny them their humanity. In other words, the black sermon as symbolic language must affirm something. This affirmation finds expression in the community's continual engagement with what it means to be human, which is inseparable from the meaning of reality. Black people continue to grapple with what it means to be black in the West, to engage the twin problems of articulating the self and imagining freedom, and to question the position of blacks in capitalism. In the context of a black American narrative code, black American fiction writers recover the sermon as a *repressed formalism.*

The grammar of the sermon is a submerged presence in African American discourse. It repeats the rhythms of plot, complication, climax, and resolution. Its end point is, as Spillers reminds us, "cathartic release . . . an instrument of a collective catharsis, binding

1. Lincoln, *Black Church since Frazier,* 122. See also Jones, *Blues People,* 42.

once again the isolated members of community."[2] The preacher through his ritual form of expression—the sermon—*structures* the meaning of blackness as he tells the story of a fallen man or woman risen. He regenerates the spirits of his downtrodden community with his meditation on freedom—freedom from sin and freedom to articulate the self.

Within the symbolic universe of the black sermon, the preacher accomplishes a mythic re-vision as well. He recalls the first movement of creation, "In the beginning . . ." Out of primordial chaos God created an orderly world and assigned a preeminent place to man and woman among His creatures. Man and woman were charged with ordering all things in this once pristine world free of racial and gender strife. In their replication of this divine act, black writers, like their preacher counterparts, call "the altered universe of the black diaspora" to order.[3] Through their incorporation of sermonic rhetoric, they echo the call of the black preacher, who steps out on space and time and boldly proclaims, "I'll make me a world."

Black writers are attracted to the sermon because it empowers blackness. It is central to the way in which a black identity is produced and reproduced when the preacher and community in unison engage in the emancipation of the self. These writers employ literary modes all reminiscent of the folk preacher and jazz musician as they draw on all segments of the literary world for their acts of literary production. Like the preacher, the writers extend and revise the nature of reality, which revolves around "the color of sin/the color of skin."[4] The tenor and tone of black American life are shaped by this discourse of difference.

The consciousness of the *difference* is always existential. Only in the expression of difference does one get back to the African modality that permits us to begin to answer the question: why do Americans of African descent do what they do? The preacher, as well as the bluesman or -woman and jazz virtuoso, is engaged in an enduring search for wholeness. The preacher's cultural productions lead horizontally back to Africa and vertically upward to

2. "Fabrics of History," 4.

3. Holloway, "*Beloved:* A Spiritual," 516.

4. Nicholas F. Gier, "The Color of Sin/The Color of Skin: Ancient Color Blindness and the Philosophical Origins of Modern Racism." See also John Hope Franklin, ed., *Color and Race.*

Heaven as they embody the community's desire to move from race to grace. Much of black American literature is infused with this search for wholeness, which has its roots in the historic black church.

In this study, I have focused on how black writers transmute the rhetorical forms that developed out of the black church into imaginative literature. They situate the sermon at the center of black American culture—even as they maintain a lover's quarrel with this conservative discourse. The writers use the sermon as a way of translating difference and as a way of insisting upon their difference, unceremoniously located at the political and rhetorical center of American discourse. In that it reflects and affects a set of particular psychic, social, and historical needs, the black sermon, at its best, stands as a central proof text in the construction of African American social reality.

We see evidence of the cultural markings of the sermon in the works of such diverse writers as Frances Ellen Watkins Harper, Jean Toomer, Zora Neale Hurston, Richard Wright, Ishmael Reed, Leon Forrest, Alice Walker, Ernest Gaines, Toni Morrison, Gloria Naylor, Julius Lester, and C. Eric Lincoln. Surveying the emotionally arid landscape of the United States, these novelists use the sermon as the basis for inventing new paradigms of self and society—an impulse engendered by the slave narratives.

Harper, for example, as a representative of the early black novelists, advocates a religious determinism, while Reed, with his irreverent satires, strives to escape religious determinism and its attendant ideological blindness. If we focus solely on whether or not a particular writer endorses the Christian model, we miss the point of how the religious orientation of Americans of African descent influences the construction of a black self. Collectively, the works of these writers present a composite "self-portrait" of a community and reveal the complexity of the black American character.

The evolution of the black novel suggests the presence of continuities that exist through the exercise of the artistic imagination. In the process, these writers reveal the complexity of the black American character. With a strong emphasis on integrationist poetics and uplift, Harper, in *Iola Leroy,* subscribes to a religious determinism as the route to the American mainstream. Toomer, Hughes, and Hurston use the sermon as a metaphorical expression between chaos and order, and between immorality and morality. They often represent the alternative visions of the spirituals and the blues as a dialogic tension between a sapient elder and a wayward child.

The division between the form and the content of black life becomes more pronounced in the works of Wright, Petry, Ellison, and Baldwin, although it retains its essential spiritual character. Against the background of a vibrant urban milieu with its emergent jazz aesthetics, we see a spiritual matrix in decline. The sacred space of the church faces steep competition from the secular space of the nightclub and street corner.

In the wake of the civil rights and women's rights movements, black writers of the 1970s and 1980s "have increased the range of their thematic concerns from the religious and political to the economic, psychological, and philosophical aspects of contemporary life."[5] We see a generational shift away from a concern with community and toward a greater emphasis on the individual. We also see a gender shift away from a male-centered to a female-centered universe.

Overlaid with a blues quality, the fictive worlds of Ernest Gaines, *In My Father's House* (1978), Leon Forrest, *Two Wings to Veil My Face* (1983), and Julius Lester, *Do Lord Remember Me* (1984), challenge religious imperialism or the tradition that elevates the preacher to a sovereign status in the community. They delve behind the attendant bravado of the sermonic rhetoric to illuminate the role of the past in shaping individual identity. In this regard, their work echoes that of Baldwin.

While the influence of the sermon is not readily apparent in the works of Ishmael Reed and Charles Johnson, we nevertheless see evidence of its cultural markings on their literary imagination in the metaphoric titles of their novels. Reed's *Mumbo Jumbo* (1972) and *Flight to Canada* (1976) and Johnson's *Middle Passage* (1990) represent the possibility for escape and transformation of a subject people. Land as a religious issue resonates in the background. Equally important, their protagonists strive to escape the frame of a repressive ideology.

Black women writers transform women from objects in male texts to subjects in theirs. They transform a patriarchal discourse and genderize God—assumed to be white, male, and distant—as female. So while we discern sermonic rhythms in the fictive worlds of Walker, Morrison, and Naylor, they have a distinctively feminine

5. Bell, *Afro-American Novel*, 278–79.

identity. They take the reader through the interiority of black life; they explore the full route to psychic freedom that the sermon provides the powerless black community. The self-voicing that emerges out of their work evinces a concern for nurturing and female independence.

And finally, in C. Eric Lincoln's *Avenue Clayton City* (1988), we have a return to a more traditional setting, the small southern town. The first novel by this noted sociologist of black religion recalls the religious determinism of Harper, with its attendant ideological blindness. We see the sermonic universe shorn of its vitality. Lincoln reduces the complexities of black life to stereotypes.

In grounding their work in the historic black church—the invisible institution—these writers convert their position as cultural interpreters into a position of authority. They use this position to articulate the black community's marginal position in the West. The preacher, as a sign of black people's subjugation and affirmation, represents the opaque community's historic struggle over language and, consequently, for self-definition. The ultimate thrust of the black sermon is Africa. It negates the tyranny of European aesthetics in a world where things African are devalued. In promoting a return to an earlier "ideology of form,"[6] these writers valorize the black preacher—even as they are skeptical of his conservative message—for his mythopoetic quality. Through his speech acts, he provides the vehicle by which the entire community of faith may participate in shaping its own history and restructuring cultural memory.

Like preachers, these black writers articulate the complicated relationship in America between historical memory (jeremiad) and the American Dream (desire). They transform historical consciousness into art, use it as a strategy for representation, and merge it with the political as they present the emergence of a self. In spite of the difference in generations and genders of the authors, their conjunction of voices attests to the validity of the experience as they articulate the central character of the experience for the corporate black community. They offer insights into the relationship between the preacher's ritual form of expression—the sermon—and black people's position in American society.

6. In *The Political Unconscious: Narrative as a Socially Symbolic Act*, Fredric R. Jameson opposes the view that literary creation can take place in isolation from its political context.

Selected Bibliography

Alho, Olli. *The Religion of the Slaves: A Study of the Religious Tradition and Behaviour of Plantation Slaves in the United States, 1830–1865.* Helsinki: Academia Scientiarum Fennica, 1975.

Allen, Shirley S. "The Ironic Voice in Baldwin's *Go Tell It on the Mountain.*" In *James Baldwin: A Critical Evaluation,* edited by Therman B. O'Daniel, 30–37. Washington, D.C.: Howard University Press, 1981.

———. "Religious Symbolism and Psychic Reality in Baldwin's *Go Tell It on the Mountain.*" *CLA Journal* 19, no. 2 (December 1975): 173–99.

Allen, William Francis, Charles Pickard Ware, and Lucy McKim Garrison, comps. *Slave Songs of the United States.* New York, 1867.

Alter, Robert, and Frank Kermode, eds. *The Literary Guide to the Bible.* Cambridge: Harvard University Press, 1987.

Andrews, William L. *Sisters of the Spirit: Three Black Women's Autobiographies of the Nineteenth Century.* Bloomington: Indiana University Press, 1986.

Awkward, Michael, ed. *New Essays on "Their Eyes Were Watching God."* Cambridge: Cambridge University Press, 1990.

Babb, Valerie Melissa. *Ernest Gaines.* Boston: Twayne, 1991.

Baer, Hans A. *The Black Spiritual Movement: A Religious Response to Racism.* Knoxville: University of Tennessee Press, 1984.

Baker, Houston A., Jr. "Belief, Theory, and Blues: Notes for a Post-Structuralist Criticism of Afro-American Literature." In *Belief vs. Theory in Black American Literary Criticism,* vol. 2 of *Studies in Black American Literature,* edited by Joe Weixlmann and Chester J. Fontenot, 5–30. Greenwood, Fla.: Penkevill, 1986.

———. *Blues, Ideology, and Afro-American Literature: A Vernacular Theory.* Chicago: University of Chicago Press, 1984.

———. *The Journey Back: Issues in Black Literature and Criticism.* Chicago: University of Chicago Press, 1980.

———. "To Move without Moving: An Analysis of Creativity and Commerce in Ralph Ellison's Trueblood Episode." *PMLA* 98, no. 5 (October 1983): 828–45.

———. *Workings of the Spirit: The Poetics of Afro-American Women's Writing.* Chicago: University of Chicago Press, 1991.

Bakhtin, M. M. *The Dialogic Imagination.* Austin: University of Texas Press, 1981.

Baldwin, James. "The Death of the Prophet." *Commentary* 9, no. 3 (March 1950): 257–61.

———. *Go Tell It on the Mountain.* New York: Knopf, 1953.

———. *Nobody Knows My Name.* New York: Dell Press, 1961.

———. *Notes of a Native Son.* Boston: Beacon Press, 1955.

Barksdale, Richard K. "Margaret Walker: Folk Orature and Historical Prophecy." In *Black American Poets Between Worlds, 1940–1960,* edited by R. Baxter Miller, 104–17. Knoxville: University of Tennessee Press, 1986.

Barthold, Bonnie. *Black Time: Fiction of Africa, the Caribbean, and the United States.* New Haven: Yale University Press, 1981.

Baym, Nina. *Woman's Fiction: A Guide to Novels by and about Women in America, 1820–1870.* Ithaca, N.Y.: Cornell University Press, 1978.

Beale, L. L. *Toward A Black Homiletic.* New York: Vantage, 1978.

Bell, Bernard W. *The Afro-American Novel and Its Tradition.* Amherst: University of Massachusetts Press, 1987.

———. *The Folk Roots of Afro-American Poetry.* Detroit: Broadside Press, 1974.

Bennett, Lerone, Jr. *The Negro Mood.* Chicago: Johnson, 1964.

Bercovitch, Sacvan. *The American Jeremiad.* Madison: University of Wisconsin Press, 1978.

Berger, Peter L., and Thomas Luckmann. *The Social Construction of Reality: A Treatise in the Sociology of Knowledge.* Garden City, N.Y.: Doubleday, 1966.

Bibb, Henry. *Narrative.* New York, 1849.

Blair, Edward P. *Abingdon Bible Handbook.* Nashville: Abingdon Press, 1975.

Blake, Susan L. "Ritual and Rationalization: Black Folklore in the Works of Ralph Ellison." *PMLA* 94, no. 1 (January 1979): 121–36.

Blake, William. *The Writings of William Blake.* Ed. Geoffrey Keynes. 3 vols. London, 1925.

Blassingame, John W. *The Slave Community.* Rev. ed. New York: Oxford University Press, 1979.

Bloom, Harold. *Agon: Towards a Theory of Revisionism.* New York: Oxford University Press, 1982.

———. *The Anxiety of Influence: A Theory of Poetry.* New York: Oxford University Press, 1973.

———. "'Before Moses Was, I Am': The Original and the Belated Testaments." In *Notebooks in Cultural Analysis.* Vol. 1. Durham, N.C., 1984.

Blount, Marcellus. "The Preacherly Text: African American Poetry and Vernacular Performance." *PMLA* 107, no. 3 (May 1992): 582–93.

Bluestein, Gene. *The Voices of the Folk: Folklore and American Literary Theory.* Amherst: University of Massachusetts Press, 1972.

Bone, Robert. *The Negro Novel in America.* New Haven: Yale University Press, 1958.

Brown, Lloyd W. "Ralph Ellison's Exhorters: The Role of Rhetoric in *Invisible Man.*" *CLA Journal* 13, no. 3 (March 1970): 289–303.

Burkhart, John E. *Worship.* Philadelphia: Westminister, 1982.

Busby, Mark. *Ralph Ellison.* Boston: Twayne/G. K. Hall, 1991.

Buttrick, David. *Homiletic: Moves and Structures.* Philadelphia: Fortress, 1987.

Byerman, Keith E. *Fingering the Jagged Grain: Tradition and Form in Recent Black Fiction.* Athens: University of Georgia Press, 1985.

Callahan, John F. *In the African-American Grain: The Pursuit of Voice in Twentieth-Century Black Fiction.* Urbana: University of Illinois Press, 1988.

———. "Chaos, Complexity and Possibility: The Historical Frequencies of Ralph Ellison." *Black American Literature Forum* 2 (1977): 130–38.

Calloway-Thomas, Carolyn, and John Louis Lucaites, eds. *Martin Luther King, Jr., and the Sermonic Power of Public Discourse.* Tuscaloosa: University of Alabama Press, 1993.

Campbell, Jane. *Mythic Black Fiction.* Knoxville: University of Tennessee Press, 1986.

Carby, Hazel V. "The Canon: Civil War and Reconstruction." *Michigan Quarterly Review* 28, no. 1 (Winter 1989): 35–43.

———. "Ideologies of Black Folk: The Historical Novel of Slavery." In *Slavery and the Literary Imagination,* edited by Deborah E. McDowell and Arnold Rampersad, 125–43. Baltimore: Johns Hopkins University Press, 1989.

———. *Reconstructing Womanhood: The Emergence of the Afro-American Woman Novelist.* New York: Oxford University Press, 1987.

Carter, Harold. *The Prayer Tradition of Black People.* Valley Forge, Pa.: Judson, 1976.

Chase, Gilbert. *America's Music: From the Pilgrims to the Present.* 2d ed. New York: McGraw-Hill, 1966.

Chase, Mary Ellen. *Life and Language in the Old Testament.* New York: Norton, 1955.

Christian, Barbara. *Black Women Novelists: The Development of a Tradition, 1892–1976.* Westport, Conn.: Greenwood Press, 1980.

———. "The Uses of History: Frances Harper's *Iola Leroy, Shadows Uplifted.*" In *Black Feminist Criticism: Perspectives on Black Women Writers,* 165–70. New York: Pergamon Press, 1985.

Clark, Kenneth B. *Dark Ghetto: Dilemmas of Social Power.* New York: Harper, 1965.

Cone, James H. *A Black Theology of Liberation.* Philadelphia: Lippincott, 1970.

———. *The Spirituals and the Blues.* New York: Seabury, 1972.

Conrad, Joseph. *A Conrad Argosy.* Comp. William McFee. Garden City, N.Y.: Doubleday, 1942.

Cooper, Barbara E. "Milkman's Search for Family in Toni Morrison's *Song of Solomon.*" *CLA Journal* 33, no. 2 (December 1989): 145–56.

Copher, Charles B. "Transforming the Land of Oppression into the Promised Land." In *Preaching the Gospel,* edited by Henry J. Young, 25–30. Philadelphia: Fortress, 1976.

Courlander, Harold. *Negro Folk Music U.S.A.* New York: Columbia University Press, 1963.

Covo, Jacqueline. *The Blinking Eye: Ralph Ellison and His American, French, German, and Italian Critics, 1952–1971.* Metuchen, N.J.: Scarecrow Press, 1974.

Cruse, Harold. *The Crisis of the Negro Intellectual.* New York: William Morrow, 1967.

Daly, Mary. *Beyond God the Father: Toward a Philosophy of Women's Liberation.* Boston: Beacon Press, 1973.

Daniel, Walter C. *Images of the Preacher in Afro-American Literature.* Washington, D.C.: University Press of America, 1981.

Dante. *Divine Comedy.* Trans. John Ciardi. New York: New American Library, 1954.

Davidson, Edward H. "'God's Well-Trodden Foot-Paths': Puritan Preaching and Sermon Form." *Texas Studies in Literature and Languages* 25 (Winter 1983): 503–27.

Davis, Gerald L. *I Got the World in Me and I Can Sing It, You Know: A Study of the Performed African-American Sermon.* Philadelphia: University of Pennsylvania Press, 1985.

Deren, Maya. *Divine Horsemen: The Living Gods of Haiti.* New York: Thamses & Hudson, 1953.

Derrida, Jacques. *Writing and Difference.* Trans. Alan Bass. Chicago: University of Chicago Press, 1978.

Dillenberger, John. "On Broadening the New Hermeneutic." In *The New Hermeneutic,* edited by James M. Robinson and John B. Cobb, Jr., 2:147–63. New York: Harper and Row, 1964.

Dirlik, Arif. "Culturalism as Hegemonic Ideology and Liberating Practice." *Culture Critique* 6 (Spring 1987): 13–50.

Dixon, Melvin. *Ride Out the Wilderness: Geography and Identity in Afro-American Literature.* Urbana: University of Illinois Press, 1987.

Douglass, Frederick. "American Slavery, American Religion, and the Free Church of Scotland." In *Speeches, Debates, and Interviews, 1841–1846,*

269–99. The Frederick Douglass Papers, Series 1, edited by John W. Blassingame. New Haven: Yale University Press, 1982.

———. "The Heroic Slave." In *Violence in the Black Imagination: Essays and Documents,* edited by Ronald T. Takaki, 37–77. Expanded edition. New York: Oxford University Press, 1993.

———. *The Life and Times of Frederick Douglass.* 1881. Rev. ed. 1892. Reprint, New York: Collier, 1962.

———. *My Bondage and My Freedom.* 1855. Reprint, edited and with an introduction by William L. Andrews, Urbana: University of Illinois Press, 1987.

———. *The Narrative of the Life of Frederick Douglass, An American Slave, Written by Himself.* 1845. Reprint, ed. Benjamin Quarles, Cambridge: Harvard University Press, 1960.

———. "The Southern Style of Preaching to Slaves." In *Speeches, Debates, and Interviews, 1841–1846.* The Frederick Douglass Papers, Series 1, edited by John W. Blassingame. New Haven: Yale University Press, 1982.

Downes, Olin, and Eli Seigmeister, comps. *A Treasury of American Songs.* 2d ed. New York: Knopf, 1940.

Drake, St. Clair, and Horace R. Cayton. *Black Metropolis.* 2 vols. 1945. Reprint, New York: Harper, 1962.

Dreer, Herman. *The Immediate Jewel of His Soul.* St. Louis, Mo.: Argus, 1919.

Drums and Shadows: Survival Studies among the Georgia Coastal Negroes. Savannah Unit of the Georgia Writers Project, Work Projects Administration: 1940. Reprint, Athens: University of Georgia Press, 1986.

Du Bois, W. E. B. *The Negro Church: Report of a Social Study Made under the Direction of Atlanta University; Together with the Proceedings of the Eighth Conference for the Study of Negro Problems, Held at Atlanta University, May 26th, 1903.* Atlanta: Atlanta University Press, 1903.

———. *The Souls of Black Folk.* 1903. Reprint, New York: Penguin, 1989.

Dunbar, Paul Laurence. *The Sport of the Gods.* 1902. Reprint, New York: Macmillan, 1970.

———. *The Uncalled.* 1898. Reprint, New York: International Association of Newspapers and Authors, 1901.

Elder, Arlene A. *The "Hindered Hand": Cultural Implications of Early African-American Fiction.* Westport, Conn.: Greenwood Press, 1978.

Eliade, Mircea. *Myths, Dreams, and Mysteries.* 1957. Reprint, New York: Harper, 1975.

———. *The Sacred and the Profane.* 1957. Reprint, New York: Harcourt, 1959.

Ellison, Ralph. *Going to the Territory.* New York: Random House, 1986.

———. *Invisible Man.* New York: Random House, 1952.

———. "Out of the Hospital and Under the Bar." In *Soon One Morning:*

New Writing by American Negroes, 1940–1962, edited by Herbert Hill. New York: Knopf, 1963.

———. *Shadow and Act.* New York: Random House, 1964.

Epstein, Dena J. *Sinful Tunes and Spirituals: Black Folk Music to the Civil War.* Urbana: University of Illinois Press, 1977.

Fauset, Arthur Huff. *Black Gods of the Metropolis: Negro Religious Cults in the Urban North.* 1944. Reprint, Philadelphia: University of Pennsylvania Press, 1971.

Felder, Cain Hope. *Troubling Biblical Waters: Race, Class, and Family.* Maryknoll, N.Y.: Orbis, 1989.

Fish, Stanley E. *Self-Consuming Artifacts.* Berkeley: University of California Press, 1972.

Foner, Philip S. *The Voice of Black America: Major Speeches by Negroes in the United States, 1797–1971.* New York: Simon and Schuster, 1972.

Fontenot, Chester J., Jr. Review of *The Craft of Ralph Ellison,* by Robert G. O'Meally. *Black American Literature Forum* 15, no. 2 (Summer 1981): 79–80.

———. "Visionaries, Mystics, and Revolutionaries: Narrative Postures in Black Fiction." In *Studies in Black American Literature,* vol. 1, *Black American Prose Theory,* edited by Joe Weixlmann and Chester J. Fontenot, Jr., 63–87. Greenwood, Fla.: Penkevill, 1984.

Forster, E. M. *Aspects of the Novel.* New York: Harcourt, Brace, 1927.

Franklin, C. L. *Give Me This Mountain: Life History and Selected Sermons.* Ed. Jeff Todd Titon. Urbana: University of Illinois Press, 1989.

Franklin, John Hope, ed. *Color and Race.* Boston: Beacon Press, 1968.

Frazier, E. Franklin. "The Failure of the Negro Intellectual." In *The Death of White Sociology,* edited by Joyce A. Ladner, 52–66. New York: Random House, 1973.

———. *The Negro Church in America.* 1963. Reprint, New York: Schocken, 1974.

Fredrickson, George M. *The Black Image in the White Mind: The Debate on Afro-American Character and Destiny, 1817–1914.* New York: Harper and Row, 1971.

Frye, Northrop. *Anatomy of Criticism.* 1957. Reprint, Princeton: Princeton University Press, 1973.

———. *Fables of Identity: Studies in Poetic Mythology.* New York: Harbinger, 1963.

———. *Fearful Symmetry.* 1947. Reprint, Princeton: Princeton University Press, 1974.

———. "Varieties of Literary Utopias." *Daedalus* 94, no. 2 (Spring 1965): 323–47.

Fulghum, W. B., Jr. *A Dictionary of Biblical Allusions in English Literature.* New York: Holt, Rinehart, and Winston, 1965.

Fullinwider, S. P. *The Mind and Mood of Black America.* Homewood, Ill.: Dorsey, 1969.

Gaines, Ernest J. *In My Father's House.* New York: Knopf, 1978.

Gates, Henry Louis., Jr. "The Blackness of Blackness: A Critique of the Sign and the Signifying Monkey." In *Black Literature and Literary Theory,* edited by Henry Louis Gates, Jr., 285–321. New York: Methuen, 1984.

———. *Figures in Black: Words, Signs, and the "Racial" Self.* New York: Oxford University Press, 1987.

———. "Preface to Blackness: Text and Pretext." In *Afro-American Literature: The Reconstruction of Instruction,* edited by Dexter Fisher and Robert B. Stepto, 44–69. New York: Modern Language Association, 1978.

———. *The Signifying Monkey: Towards a Theory of Afro-American Literary Criticism.* New York: Oxford University Press, 1988.

Geertz, Clifford. *The Interpretation of Cultures.* New York: Basic Books, 1973.

Genovese, Eugene D. *Roll, Jordan, Roll: The World the Slaves Made.* New York: Pantheon, 1974.

Gier, Nicholas F. "The Color of Sin/The Color of Skin: Ancient Color Blindness and the Philosophical Origins of Modern Racism." *The Journal of Religious Thought* 46, no. 1 (Summer–Fall 1989): 42–52.

Greeley, Andrew M. *Religion: A Secular Theory.* New York: Free Press/Macmillan, 1982.

Grimstead, David. "Melodrama as Echo of the Historically Voiceless." In *Anonymous Americans,* edited by Tamara K. Hareven. Englewood Cliffs, N.J.: Prentice-Hall, 1971.

Gutman, Herbert G. *The Black Family in Slavery and Freedom, 1750–1925.* New York: Vintage, 1976.

Hamilton, Charles V. *The Black Preacher in America.* New York: William Morrow, 1972.

Harding, Vincent. *There Is a River: The Black Struggle for Freedom in America.* New York: Harcourt, Brace, Jovanovich, 1981.

Harper, Frances Ellen Watkins. *Iola Leroy.* 1892. Reprint, Boston: Beacon Press, 1987.

Harris, Sara. *Father Divine.* 1953. Reprint, New York: Macmillan, 1971.

Harris, Trudier. *Black Women in the Fiction of James Baldwin.* Knoxville: University of Tennessee Press, 1985.

———. "From Exile to Asylum: Religion and Community in the Writings of Contemporary Black Women." In *Women's Writing in Exile,* edited by Mary Lynn Broe and Angela Ingram, 151–69. Chapel Hill: University of North Carolina Press, 1989.

———. "Three Black Women Writers and Humanism: A Folk Perspective." In *Black American Literature and Humanism,* edited by R. Baxter Miller, 50–74. Lexington: University Press of Kentucky, 1981.

Hatcher, William E. *John Jasper: The Unmatched Negro Philosopher and Preacher.* 1908. Reprint, New York: Negro Universities Press, 1969.

Hedin, Raymond. "Strategies of Form in the American Slave Narrative." In *The Art of Slave Narrative,* edited by John Sekora and Darwin T. Turner, 25–35. Macomb: Western Illinois University Press, Essays in Literature, 1982.

Hemenway, Robert E. *Zora Neale Hurston: A Literary Biography.* Urbana: University of Illinois Press, 1977.

Henderson, Stephen. "The Heavy Blues of Sterling Brown: A Study of Craft and Tradition." *Black American Literature Forum* 14, no. 1 (Spring 1980): 32–44.

———. *Understanding the New Black Poetry: Black Speech and Black Music as Poetic References.* New York: William Morrow, 1972.

———. "Worrying the Line: Notes on Black American Poetry." In *The Line in Postmodern Poetry,* edited by Robert Frank and Henry Sayre, 60–82. Urbana: University of Illinois Press, 1988.

Herskovits, Melville J. *The Myth of the Negro Past.* New York: Harper, 1941.

Hesiod. *Poems.* Trans. R. M. Frazer. Norman: University of Oklahoma Press, 1983.

Higginbotham, A. Leon, Jr. *In the Matter of Color: Race and the American Legal Process—The Colonial Period.* Oxford: Oxford University Press, 1978.

Holloway, Karla F. C. "*Beloved:* A Spiritual." *Callaloo* 13, no. 3 (Summer 1990): 516–25.

Holloway, Karla F. C., and S. Demetrakopoulos. *New Dimensions of Spirituality: A BiRacial and BiCultural Reading of the Novels of Toni Morrison.* Westport, Conn.: Greenwood Press, 1987.

Holt, Grace Sims. "Stylin' Outta the Black Pulpit." In *Rappin' and Stylin' Out: Communication in Urbana Black America,* edited by Thomas Kochman. Urbana: University of Illinois Press, 1972.

Hovet, Grace Ann, and Barbara Lounsberry. "Flying as Symbol and Legend in Toni Morrison's *The Bluest Eye, Sula,* and *Song of Solomon.*" *CLA Journal* 27.2 (December 1983): 119, 140.

Howard, Lillie P. *Zora Neale Hurston.* Boston: Twayne/G. K. Hall, 1980.

Hubbard, Dolan. "Call and Response: Intertextuality in the Poetry of Langston Hughes and Margaret Walker." *Langston Hughes Review* 7, no. 1 (Spring 1988): 22–30.

———. "David Walker's *Appeal* and the American Puritan Jeremiadic Tradition." *Centennial Review* 30, no. 3 (Summer 1986): 331–46.

———. "In Quest of Authority: Toni Morrison's *Song of Solomon* and the Rhetoric of the Black Preacher." *College Language Association Journal* 35, no. 3 (March 1982): 288–302.

Hubbard, Dolan, and Bernard H. Sullivan, Jr., "'Let My People Go': A

Spiritually Charged Mascon of Hope and Liberation." *The A.M.E. Zion Quarterly Review* 97, no. 3 (October 1985): 18–28.

Huggins, Nathan Irvin, Martin Kilson, and Daniel M. Fox, eds. *Key Issues in the Afro-American Experience.* 2 vols. New York: Harcourt Brace Jovanovich, 1971.

Hughes, Langston. "The Negro Artist and the Racial Mountain." 1926. In *Voices from the Harlem Renaissance,* edited by Nathan Irvin Huggins, 305–9. New York: Oxford University Press, 1976.

———. *Not without Laughter.* 1930. Reprint, New York: Macmillan, 1969.

Hughes, Langston, and Arna Bontemps, comps. *The Book of Negro Folklore.* 1958. Reprint, New York: Dodd, Mead, 1983.

Hurston, Zora Neale. *Jonah's Gourd Vine.* 1934. Reprint, Philadelphia: Lippincott, 1971.

———. *The Sanctified Church.* Berkeley, Calif.: Turtle Island, 1983.

———. *Their Eyes Were Watching God.* 1937. Reprint, New York: Harper and Row, 1990.

Hymes, Dell H. "The Ethnography of Speaking." In *Readings in The Sociology of Language,* edited by Joshua Fishman, 99–138. The Hague: Mouton, 1969.

Iser, Wolfgang. "The Reading Process: A Phenomenological Approach." In *The Implied Reader,* 274–94. Baltimore: Johns Hopkins University Press, 1974.

Jackson, Blyden. "The Ghetto of the Negro Novel: A Theme with Variations." In *The Waiting Years: Essays on American Negro Literature,* 179–88. Baton Rouge: Louisiana State University Press, 1976.

———. *The Long Beginning, 1746–1895.* Vol. 1 of *A History of Afro-American Literature.* Baton Rouge: Louisiana State University Press, 1989.

Jacobs, Harriet. *Incidents in the Life of a Slave Girl.* Ed. Jean Fagan Yellin. 1861. Reprint, Cambridge: Harvard University Press, 1987.

Jameson, Fredric R. *The Political Unconscious: Narrative as a Socially Symbolic Act.* Ithaca, N.Y.: Cornell University Press, 1981.

———. *The Prison-House of Language.* Princeton: Princeton University Press, 1972.

Johnson, Charles S. *The Shadow of the Plantation.* Chicago: University of Chicago Press, 1934.

Johnson, James Weldon. *Along This Way.* New York: Viking, 1933.

———. *The Autobiography of an Ex-Coloured Man.* 1912. Reprint, New York: Hill and Wang, 1960.

———. *God's Trombones: Seven Negro Sermons in Verse.* 1927. Reprint, New York: Penguin, 1981.

———. "Lift Every Voice and Sing." 1927. In *Songs of Zion,* 32- 33. Nashville: Abingdon, 1981.

———. "Preface to the First Edition of *The Book of American Negro Poetry*." 1922. In *Voices from the Harlem Renaissance*, edited by Nathan Irvin Huggins, 281–304. New York: Oxford University Press, 1976.

Johnson, James Weldon, comp. *The Book of American Negro Poetry*. 1922. Reprint, New York: Harcourt, 1931.

Johnson, James Weldon, and J. Rosamond Johnson, comps. *The Books of American Negro Spirituals*. 2 vols. 1925, 1926. Reprint, New York: Viking, 1969.

Jones, LeRoi. *Blues People*. New York: William Morrow, 1963.

———. *The System of Dante's Hell*. New York: Grove Press, 1966.

Jones, Major. *Black Awareness*. Nashville: Abingdon, 1971.

Keil, Charles. *Urban Blues*. Chicago: University of Chicago Press, 1966.

Kennedy, George A. *New Testament Interpretation through Rhetorical Criticism*. Chapel Hill: University of North Carolina Press, 1984.

Kent, George E. "Baldwin and the Problem of Being." In *James Baldwin: A Critical Evaluation*, edited by Therman B. O'Daniel, 19–29. Washington, D.C.: Howard University Press, 1977.

———. "Ralph Ellison and Afro-American Cultural Tradition." In *Speaking for You: The Vision of Ralph Ellison*, edited by Kimberly W. Benston, 95–104. Washington, D.C.: Howard University Press, 1987.

———. "Reflections on Stephen Henderson's *Understanding the New Black Poetry*, A Review-Essay." *Black World* 23, no. 4 (February 1974): 51–52, 73–86.

Kermode, Frank. "John." In *The Literary Guide to the Bible*, edited by Robert Alter and Frank Kermode, 440–66. Cambridge: Harvard University Press, 1987.

———. *The Sense of an Ending*. Oxford: Oxford University Press, 1966.

King, Martin Luther, Jr., *Strength to Love*. 1963. Reprint, Philadelphia: Fortress, 1981.

———. *Stride toward Freedom: The Montgomery Story*. New York: Harper, 1958.

Krasner, James. "Zora Neale Hurston and Female Autobiography." *Black American Literature Forum* 23, no. 1 (Spring 1989): 113–26.

Kummel, W. G. *Introduction to the New Testament*. 17th ed. Trans. Howard Clark Kee. London: Abingdon, 1975.

Lanternari, Vittorio. *The Religions of the Oppressed*. New York: Knopf, 1963.

Laymon, Charles M., ed. *The Interpreter's One-Volume Commentary on the Bible*. Nashville: Abindgon, 1971.

Le Barre, Weston. *The Ghost Dance: Origins of Religion*. New York: Doubleday, 1970.

Lester, Julius. *Do Lord Remember Me*. New York: Holt, Rinehart, and Winston, 1985.

Levine, Lawrence W. *Black Culture and Black Consciousness: Afro-American Folk Thought from Slavery to Freedom.* Oxford: Oxford University Press, 1977.

Lewis, David L. *King: A Biography.* 2d ed. Urbana: University of Illinois Press, 1978.

Lincoln, C. Eric, and Lawrence H. Mamiya. *The Black Church in the African American Experience.* Durham: Duke University Press, 1990.

———. *The Black Church since Frazier.* New York: Shocken, 1974.

———. *Race, Religion, and the Continuing American Dilemma.* New York: Hill and Wang, 1984.

Locke, Alain. *Negro Art: Past and Present.* Washington, D.C.: Associates in Negro Folk Education, 1936.

———. "The New Negro." In *The New Negro,* edited by Alain Locke, 3–16. 1925. Reprint, New York: Atheneum, 1980.

Loewenberg, Bert James, and Ruth Bogin. *Black Women in Nineteenth Century American Life.* State College: Pennsylvania State University Press, 1976.

Long, Charles H. *Significations: Signs, Symbols, and Images in the Interpretation of Religion.* Philadelphia: Fortress, 1986.

Lovell, John, Jr. *Black Song: The Forge and the Flame.* New York: Paragon, 1986.

———. "The Social Implications of the Negro Spiritual." In *The Social Implications of Early Negro Music in the United States,* edited by Bernard Katz, 128–37. New York: Arno/New York Times, 1969.

McDowell, Deborah E. "'The Changing Same': Generational Connections and Black Women Novelists." *New Literary History* 18.2 (Winter 1987): 281–302.

Macebuh, Stanley. *James Baldwin: A Critical Study.* New York: Third Press/Joseph Okpaku, 1973.

MacLean, Gilmour S. "The Revelation to John." In *The Interpreter's One-Volume Commentary on the Bible,* edited by Charles M. Laymon, 945–68. Nashville: Abingdon Press, 1971.

Mapson, J. Wendell, Jr. *The Ministry of Music in the Black Church.* Valley Forge, Pa.: Judson, 1984.

Marty, Martin E. "Martin Luther King: The Preacher as Virtuoso." *Christian Century* 106, no. 11 (April 5, 1989): 348–50.

Massey, James Earl. *Designing the Sermon: Order and Movement in Preaching.* Nashville: Abingdon, 1980.

Mays, Benjamin E. *The Negro's God as Reflected in His Literature.* 1938. Reprint, New York: Atheneum, 1968.

Mbiti, John S. *African Religions and Philosophy.* Garden City, N.Y.: Anchor/Doubleday, 1969.

Mellard, James M. "The Popular Mode in Narrative." In *Four Modes: A Rhetoric of Modern Fiction,* edited by James M. Mellard. New York: Macmillan, 1973.

Miller, R. Baxter. "'Does Man Love Art?': The Humanistic Aesthetic of Gwendolyn Brooks." In *Black American Literature and Humanism,* edited by R. Baxter Miller, 95–112. Lexington: University Press of Kentucky, 1981.

Millet, Kate. *Sexual Politics.* 1969. Reprint, New York: Touchstone, 1990.

Mitchell, Henry H. *Black Preaching.* New York: Harper, 1970.

———. *The Recovery of Preaching.* New York: Harper, 1977.

Morrison, Toni. *Beloved.* New York: Knopf, 1987.

———. "Rootedness: The Ancestor as Foundation." In *Black Women Writers (1950–1980): A Critical Evaluation,* edited by Mari Evans, 339–45. Garden City, N.Y.: Anchor/Doubleday, 1984.

———. *Song of Solomon.* 1977. Reprint, New York: Plume, 1987.

Moses, Wilson Jeremiah. *Black Messiahs and Uncle Toms: Social and Literary Manipulations of a Religious Myth.* University Park: Pennsylvania State University Press, 1982.

———. "The Lost World of the Negro, 1895–1919: Black Literary and Intellectual Life before the 'Renaissance.'" *Black American Literature Forum* 21, nos. 1–2 (Spring–Summer 1987): 61–84.

Moyd, Olin P. *Redemption in Black Theology.* Valley Forge, Pa.: Judson, 1979.

Nadel, Alan. *Ralph Ellison and the American Canon.* Iowa City: University of Iowa Press, 1988.

Naylor, Gloria. *Linden Hills.* New York: Penguin, 1985.

Oakley, Giles. *The Devil's Music: A History of the Blues.* New York: Taplinger, 1976.

O'Meally, Robert G. "Frederick Douglass' 1845 *Narrative:* The Text Was Meant to Be Preached." In *Afro-American Literature: The Reconstruction of Instruction,* edited by Dexter Fisher and Robert B. Stepto, 192–211. New York: MLA, 1978.

———. Introduction to *New Essays on "Invisible Man,"* edited by Robert G. O'Meally. Cambridge: Cambridge University Press, 1988.

Ong, Walter. *Orality and Literacy: The Technology of the Word.* New York: Methuen, 1983.

Otten, Terry. *The Crime of Innocence in the Fiction of Toni Morrison.* Columbia: University of Missouri Press, 1989.

Otto, Rudolf. *The Idea of the Holy.* 1917. Trans. John W. Harvey. Rev. ed. London: Oxford University Press, 1936.

The Oxford Annotated Bible. Revised Standard Version. New York: Oxford University Press, 1962.

Palosaari, Ronald Gerald. "The Image of the Black Minister in the Black Novel from Dunbar to Baldwin." Ph.D. diss., University of Minnesota, 1970.

Paris, Arthur E. *Black Pentecostalism: Southern Religion in an Urban World.* Amherst: University of Massachusetts Press, 1982.

Paris, Peter J. *Black Leaders in Conflict: Joseph H. Jackson, Martin Luther King, Jr., Malcolm X, and Adam Clayton Powell, Jr.* New York: Pilgrim Press, 1978.

Payne, Daniel. *Recollections of Seventy Years.* Nashville: A.M.E. Sunday School Union, 1888.

Payne, Ladell. *Black Novelists and the Southern Literary Tradition.* Athens: University of Georgia Press, 1981.

Perry, Menakhem. "Literary Dynamics: How the Order of a Text Creates Its Meaning." *Poetics Today* 1, nos. 1–2 (Autumn 1979): 350–64.

Petesch, Donald A. *A Spy in the Enemy's Country: The Emergence of Modern Black Literature.* Iowa City: University of Iowa Press, 1989.

Pipes, William H. *Say Amen, Brother.* New York: The William-Frederick Press, 1951.

Pitts, Walter. "West African Poetics in the Black Preaching Style." *American Speech* 64, no. 2 (1989): 137–49.

Plato. *Dialogues.* Vol. 1. Trans. B. Jowett. 4th ed. Oxford: Oxford University Press, 1953.

Preston, Dickinson J. *Young Frederick Douglass: The Maryland Years.* Baltimore: Johns Hopkins University Press, 1980.

Raboteau, Albert J. *Slave Religion: The "Invisible Institution" in the Antebellum South.* Oxford: Oxford University Press, 1978.

Radin, Paul. "Status, Phantasy, and the Christian Dogma." In *God Struck Me Dead,* iv–ix. Vol. 19 of *The American Slave: A Composite Autobiography,* gen. ed. George P. Rawick. Westport, Conn.: Greenwood Press, 1971.

Ray, Sandy F. "Elements in Black Preaching." *The Journal of Religious Thought* 30, no. 1 (Spring–Summer 1973).

Raymond, Charles A. "The Religious Life of the Negro Slave." *Harper's New Monthly Magazine* 27, no. 160 (September 1863): 479–85; 27, no. 161 (October 1863): 676–82; 27, no. 162 (November 1863): 816–25.

Roberts, J. Deotis. "The Black Caucus and the Failure of Theology." *The Journal of Religious Thought* 26, no. 2 (Summer Supplement 1969): 15–25.

Robinson, Douglas. *American Apocalypses: The Image of the End of the World in American Literature.* Baltimore: Johns Hopkins University Press, 1985.

Rosenburg, Bruce A. *The Art of the American Folk Preacher.* New York: Oxford University Press, 1970.

Rosenburg, Ruth. "And the Children May Know Their Names: Toni Morrison's *Song of Solomon.*" *Literary Onomastics Studies* 8 (1981).

Saldivar, Ramon. *Figural Language in the Novel: The Flowers of Speech from Cervantes to Joyce.* Princeton: Princeton University Press, 1984.

Scholes, Robert, and Robert Kellogg. *The Nature of Narrative.* New York: Oxford University Press, 1966.

Scott, Nathan A., Jr. "Judgment Marked by a Cellar: The American Negro Writer and the Dialectic of Despair." *Denver Quarterly* 2, no. 2 (Summer 1967): 5–35.

Sernett, Milton C. *Black Religion and American Evangelicalism.* Metuchen, N.J.: Scarecrow Press, 1975.

Shange, Ntozake. *For Colored Girls Who Have Considered Suicide When the Rainbow Is Enuf.* New York: Macmillan, 1975.

Shorter, Aylward. *African Christian Theology.* Maryknoll, N.Y.: Orbis, 1977.

Shulman, Robert. *Social Criticism and Nineteenth-Century American Fictions.* Columbia: University of Missouri Press, 1987.

Smith, David. "Not to Need Permission for Desire—Well Now, That *Was* Freedom." Review of *Beloved,* by Toni Morrison. *America* (Feb. 20, 1988): 197.

Smith, Valerie. "The Meaning of Narration in *Invisible Man.*" In *New Essays on "Invisible Man,"* edited by Robert O'Meally, 25–53. Cambridge: Cambridge University Press, 1988.

———. *Self-Discovery and Authority in Afro-American Narrative.* Cambridge: Harvard University Press, 1987.

Smitherman, Geneva. *Talkin' and Testifyin': The Language of Black America.* Boston: Houghton Mifflin, 1977.

Southern, Eileen. *The Music of Black Americans.* New York: Norton, 1971.

Spillers, Hortense J. "Fabrics of History: Essays on the Black Sermon." Ph.D. diss., Brandeis, 1974.

———. "Martin Luther King and the Style of the Black Sermon." In *The Black Experience in Religion,* edited by C. Eric Lincoln, 77–98. New York: Anchor, 1974.

———. "'The Permanent Obliquity of an In(pha)llibly Straight': In the Time of the Daughters and the Fathers." In *Changing Our Own Words,* edited by Cheryl A. Wall, 127–49. New Brunswick, N.J.: Rutgers University Press, 1989.

Stepto, Robert B. *From Behind the Veil: A Study of Afro-American Narrative.* Urbana: University of Illinois Press, 1979.

Strout, Cushing. *Making American Tradition: Visions and Revisions from Ben*

Franklin to Alice Walker. New Brunswick, N.J.: Rutgers University Press, 1990.

Stuckey, Sterling. "Through the Prism of Folklore: The Black Ethos in Slavery." In *Black and White in American Culture,* edited by Jules Chametzky and Sidney Kaplan, 172–91. Amherst: University of Massachusetts Press, 1969.

The Student Peace Union, comp. *Songs for Peace.* New York: Oak Publications, 1966.

Sylvander, Carolyn Wedin. *James Baldwin.* New York: Frederick Ungar, 1980.

———. "Ralph Ellison's *Invisible Man* and Female Stereotypes." *Black American Literature Forum* 9, no. 3 (1975): 77–79.

Tate, Claudia. *Domestic Allegories of Political Desire: The Black Heroine's Text at the Turn of the Century.* New York: Oxford University Press, 1992.

———. "Notes on the Invisible Women in Ralph Ellison's *Invisible Man.*" In *Speaking for You: The Vision of Ralph Ellison,* edited by Kimberly W. Benston, 163–72. Washington, D.C.: Howard University Press, 1987.

Thelwell, Mike. "Back with the Wind: Mr. Styron and the Reverend Turner." In *William Styron's Nat Turner: Ten Black Writers Respond,* edited by John Henrik Clarke, 79–91. Boston: Beacon Press, 1968.

Thurman, Howard. *Deep River* and *The Negro Spiritual Speaks of Life and Death.* 1945, 1955. Reprint, Richmond, Ind.: Friends United, 1975.

Thurman, Wallace, with William Jourdan Rapp. *Harlem.* New York, 1929.

Titon, Jeff Todd. *Early Down Home Blues: A Musical and Cultural Analysis.* Urbana: University of Illinois Press, 1977.

Toomer, Jean. *Cane.* 1923. Reprint, New York: Norton, 1988.

Trilling, Lionel. *The Liberal Imagination.* 1950. Reprint, London: Secker and Warburg, 1955.

Trimmer, Joseph F. *A Casebook on Ralph Ellison's "Invisible Man."* New York: Thomas Y. Crowell, 1972.

Turner, Darwin T. *In a Minor Chord: Three Afro-American Writers and Their Search for Identity.* Carbondale: Southern Illinois University Press, 1971.

———. "Theme, Characterization, and Style in the Works of Toni Morrison." In *Black Women Writers,* edited by Mari Evans, 361–69. Garden City, N.Y.: Anchor/Doubleday, 1984.

Turner, Denys. *Marxism and Christianity.* Oxford: Basil Blackwell, 1983.

Turner, Victor. *Dramas, Fields, and Metaphors.* Ithaca, N.Y.: Cornell University Press, 1974.

Vivas, Eliseo. "The Object of the Poem." In *Critical Theory since Plato,* edited by Hazard Adams, 1069–77. New York: Harcourt, 1971.

Walker, Alice. *In Search of Our Mother's Garden.* New York: Harcourt, 1984.

Walker, Wyatt Tee. *"Somebody's Calling My Name": Black Sacred Music and Social Change.* Valley Forge, Pa.: Judson, 1979.

———. *The Soul of Black Worship, A Trilogy: Praying, Preaching, Singing.* New York: Martin Luther King Fellows Press, 1984.

Washington, Booker T. *The Future of the American Negro.* Boston: Small, Maynard, 1899.

———. *A New Negro for a New Century.* 1900. Reprint, Miami: Mnemosyne, 1969.

Washington, James M. "The Origins and Emergence of Black Baptist Separatism, 1863–1897." Ph.D. diss., Yale University, 1979.

Washington, Joseph R., Jr. "Folk Religion and Negro Congregations: The Fifth Religion." In *African American Religious Studies: An Interdisciplinary Anthology,* edited by Gayraud Wilmore, 50–59. Durham, N.C.: Duke University Press, 1989.

West, Cornel. *Prophecy Deliverance!: An Afro-American Revolutionary Christianity.* Philadelphia: Westminster Press, 1982.

Whalum, Wendall. "Black Hymnody." *Review and Expositor* 70, no. 3 (Summer 1973): 341–55.

Whalum, Wendall, David Baker, and Richard Long. "Afro-American Music." In *The Black American Reference Book,* edited by Mabel M. Smythe, 791–826. Englewood Cliffs, N.J.: Prentice Hall, 1976.

White, Hayden. *The Content of the Form: Narrative Discourse and Historical Representation.* Baltimore: Johns Hopkins University Press, 1987.

Williams, Sherly Anne. "The Blues Roots of Contemporary Afro-American Poetry." In *Afro-American Literature: The Reconstruction of Instruction,* edited by Dexter Fisher and Robert B. Stepto, 72–87. New York: MLA, 1979.

———. *Give Birth to Brightness: A Thematic Study in Neo-Black Literature.* New York: Dial Press, 1972.

Willis, Susan. "Eruptions of Funk: Historicizing Toni Morrison." *Black American Literature Forum* 16 (1982): 34–42.

Wills, Gary. *Inventing America: Jefferson's Declaration of Independence.* Garden City, N.Y.: Doubleday, 1978.

Wilmore, Gayraud S., Jr. "Black Theology." In *Best Black Sermons,* edited by William M. Philpot, 87–94. Valley Forge, Pa.: Judson, 1972.

———. *Black Religion and Black Radicalism.* New York: Doubleday, 1972.

Wilmore, Gayraud S., Jr., and James H. Cone, eds. *Black Theology: A Documentary History, 1966–1979.* Maryknoll, N.Y.: Orbis, 1979.

Wilson, William J. *Power, Racism, and Privilege: Race Relations in Theoretical and Sociohistorical Perspectives.* 1973. Reprint, New York: Free Press, 1976.

Woodson, Carter G. *The History of the Negro Church.* Washington, D.C.: Associated Publishers, 1921.

Work, John W. *American Negro Songs and Spirituals.* New York: Crown, 1940.

Wright, Fred. *Manners and Culture of Bible Lands.* Chicago: Moody, 1953.

Wright, Richard. "The Literature of the Negro in the United States." In *White Man, Listen!* 69–105. 1957. Reprint, Garden City, N.Y.: Anchor/Doubleday, 1964.

———. *Twelve Million Black Voices.* New York: Viking, 1941.

Index

Permissions

Excerpts from the following copyrighted works have been reprinted by permission:

"'Ah Said Ah'd Save De Text for You': Recontextualizing the Sermon to Tell (Her) Story in Zora Neale Hurston's *Their Eyes Were Watching God*," by Dolan Hubbard, reprinted from *African American Review* 27, no. 2 (Summer 1993).

"The Creation," from *God's Trombones*, by James Weldon Johnson. Copyright © 1927 by The Viking Press, Inc.; renewed © 1955 by Grace Nail Johnson. Used by permission of Viking Penguin, a division of Penguin Books USA Inc.

Go Tell It on the Mountain, by James Baldwin. Copyright © 1952, 1953 by James Baldwin. Used by permission of Doubleday, a division of Bantam Doubleday Dell Publishing Group, Inc.

"In Quest of Authority: Toni Morrison's *Song of Solomon* and the Rhetoric of the Black Preacher," by Dolan Hubbard, *CLA Journal* 35, no. 3 (March 1992): 288–302.

Invisible Man, by Ralph Ellison. Copyright © 1947, 1948, 1952 by Ralph Ellison. Reprinted by permission of Random House, Inc.

Life and Times of Frederick Douglass, by Frederick Douglass. Copyright © 1962 by Macmillan Publishing Co., Inc. Reprinted by permission of Collier Books/Macmillan.

Song of Solomon and *Beloved,* by Toni Morrison. Reprinted by permission of International Creative Management, Inc. Copyright 1977 by Toni Morrison.

Their Eyes Were Watching God, by Zora Neale Hurston. Copyright © 1937 by Harper & Row Publishers, Inc. Renewed © 1965 by John C. Hurston and Joel Hurston. Reprinted by permission of HarperCollins Publishers, Inc., and Virago Press Limited, London.

DI